Essential Audition Songs

male & female Vocalists

wannabe pop stars

International Music Publications

Series Editor: Chris Harvey

Editorial, Production and Recording: Artemis Music Limited
Design and Production: Space DPS Limited

Published 2002

RESPECT THE VALUE OF MUSIC

£16-50

Angels

Words and Music by Robert Williams and Guy Chambers

with love. And as the feel-ing grows she brings

flesh to my bones. And when love is dead, I'm lov-ing an-gels in-stead. And through it all

Anything Is Possible

Words and Music by Cathy Dennis and Chris Braide

Backing

Back For Good

Words and Music by Gary Barlow

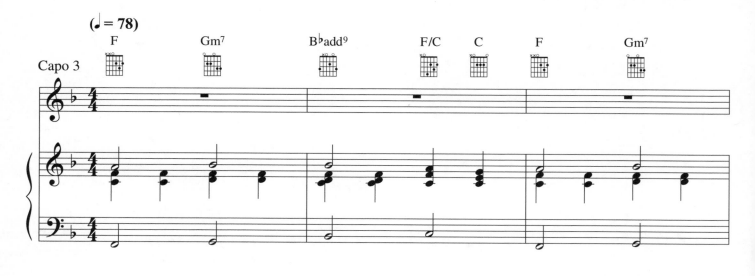

I guess____ now it's time____
Un-a-ware but un-der-lined,

for me to give up,____ I feel it's time.
I fi-gured out this sto-ry, It was-n't good,

14

never be un-co-vered a-gain.___ What-

-ev-er I said, what-ev-er I did___ I did-n't mean it,____ I just want you back for

good.___ (want you back, want you back, want you back for good.)___ When-

-ev-er I'm wrong, just tell me the song,___ and I'll sing___ it,___ you'll be right and un-der-

Backing

Ev'ry Time We Say Goodbye

Words and Music by Cole Porter

♩ = 80 Steady swing ballad

Ev-'ry time____ we say good-bye____ I die a lit-tle, ev-'ry time____ we say good-bye I won-der why a lit-tle. Why the gods a-bove me, who must be in the know, think so lit-tle of me, They al-

Get Happy

Backing

Words and Music by Harold Arlen and Ted Koehler

Backing

Flying Without Wings

Words and Music by Steve Mac and Wayne Hector

Backing

Genie In A Bottle

Words and Music by Pam Sheyne,
David Frank and Steve Kipner

Backing

Reach

Words and Music by Cathy Dennis and Andrew Todd

Lyrics:
1.(F) When the world leaves you feel-ing blue you can count on me.
2.(M) There's a place wait-ing just for you. It's a spe-cial place where your dreams all come true.

I will be there for you.

Backing

Up On The Roof

Words and Music by Gerry Goffin and Carole King

night the stars put on a show for free,_____ and

dar - ling you can share it all___ with me._____ I keep on tell - in' you, a

Backing

Whole Again

Words and Music by Andrew McCluskey, Stuart Kershaw,
Bill Padley and Jeremy Godfrey

Ba - by you're the one, you_ still turn me on,_ and you can make me

whole_ a - gain._

Spoken: For now I'll have to wait, but baby if you change your mind, don't be too late, 'cos I just can't go on,

it's already been too long, but you can make me whole again.

Karaoke Classics
9696A   PVG/CD   ISBN: 1-84328-202-X

Back For Good - Delilah - Hey Baby - I Will
Always Love You - I Will Survive - Let Me
Entertain You - Reach - New York, New York -
Summer Nights - Wild Thing

Party Hits
9499A   PVG/CD   ISBN: 1-84328-097-8

Come On Eileen - Dancing Queen - Groove Is In
The Heart - Hi Ho Silver Lining - Holiday - House
Of Fun - The Loco-Motion - Love Shack - Staying
Alive - Walking On Sunshine

Disco
9493A   PVG/CD   ISBN: 1-84328-091-4

I Feel Love - I Will Survive - I'm So Excited - Lady
Marmalade - Le Freak - Never Can Say Goodbye
- On The Radio - Relight My - Fire - YMCA - You
Sexy Thing

School Disco
9709A   PVG/CD   ISBN: 1-84328-212-7

Baggy Trousers – Club Tropicana – December
1963 (Oh What A Night) – The Final Countdown –
Karma Chameleon – The One And Only – Material
Girl – Relax – Stand And Deliver – Take On Me

The World To

Compiled by Charles Thornford

Schofield & Sims Ltd Huddersfield

The World Today

Contents

0 7217 1074 3
0 7217 1076 x Net Edition

First printed 1992

Also available from
Schofield & Sims Ltd:
The World Today Exercises
0 7217 1075 1

Printed in England by Garnett-Dickinson Print Ltd.
Artwork by Graphic Art Concepts, Leeds

The place of our World in the solar system

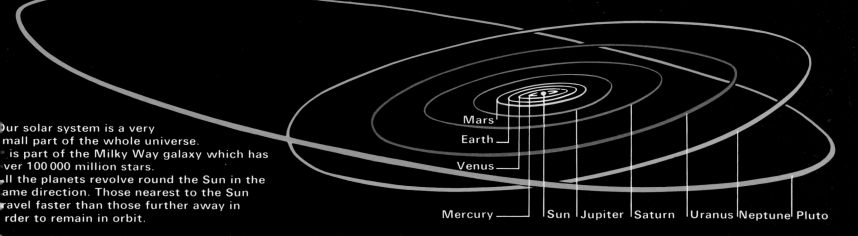

Our solar system is a very small part of the whole universe. It is part of the Milky Way galaxy which has over 100 000 million stars. All the planets revolve round the Sun in the same direction. Those nearest to the Sun travel faster than those further away in order to remain in orbit.

Mars
Earth
Venus

Mercury — Sun Jupiter Saturn Uranus Neptune Pluto

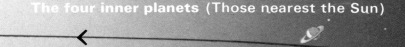

The four inner planets (Those nearest the Sun)

Mars
228 million km from the Sun, takes 1 year 322 days to travel round the Sun.

Mercury
58 million km from the Sun, takes 88 days to travel round the Sun.

Venus
108 million km from the Sun, takes 225 days to travel round the Sun.

Earth
150 million km from the Sun.
This is our World.
The Earth takes 1 year to travel round the Sun at 30 km every second.

The Moon
is 384 400 km from the Earth.
The Earth is 25 times as large as the Moon.

The Sun
is over 300 000 times as big as the Earth.

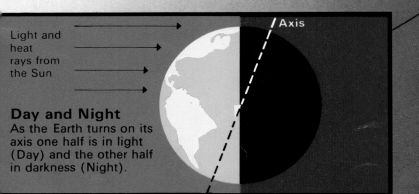

Light and heat rays from the Sun

Axis

Day and Night
As the Earth turns on its axis one half is in light (Day) and the other half in darkness (Night).

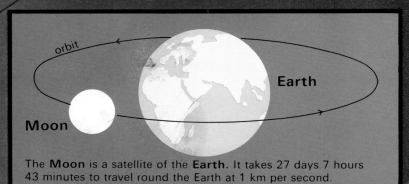

orbit

Earth

Moon

The **Moon** is a satellite of the **Earth**. It takes 27 days 7 hours 43 minutes to travel round the Earth at 1 km per second.

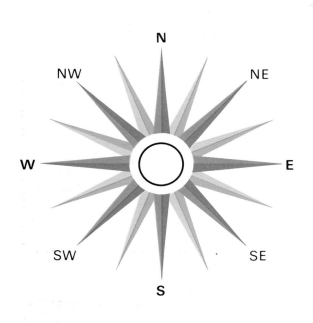

N
NW   NE
W   E
SW   SE
S

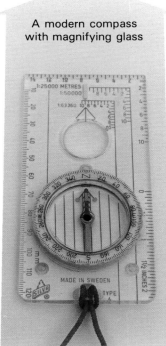

A modern compass
with magnifying glass

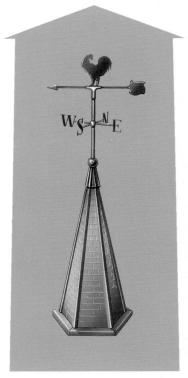

To find North

a Use a compass.
Hold your compass level and
clear of any metal objects.
Its needle will point to **North**.

b Look at a weather vane.
This has four fixed arms and
North is clearly marked on
one of them.

c If at noon (GMT) you st
with your back to the su
your shadow points to
North.

Directions from the British Isles

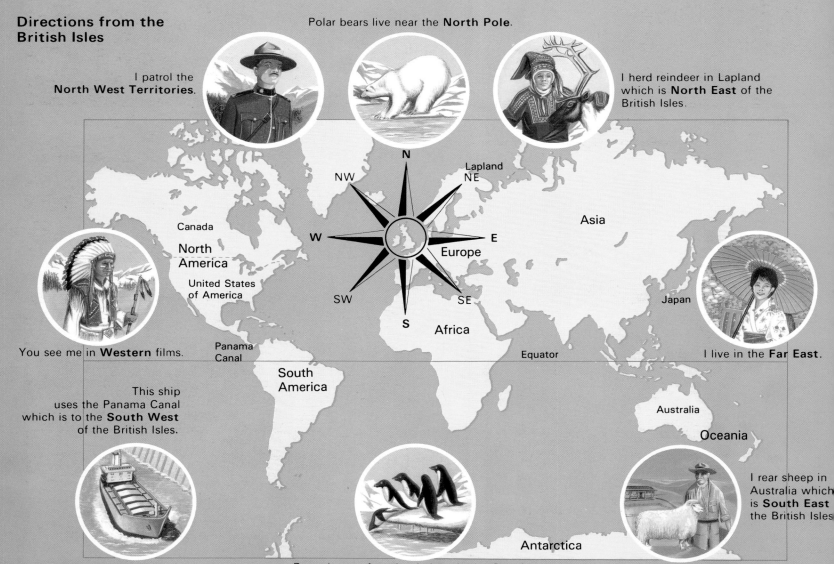

Polar bears live near the **North Pole**.

I patrol the
North West Territories.

I herd reindeer in Lapland
which is **North East** of the
British Isles.

Canada

North
America

United States
of America

You see me in **Western** films.

Panama
Canal

This ship
uses the Panama Canal
which is to the **South West**
of the British Isles.

NW   N   Lapland
                   NE
W   E
                   Europe
SW   SE
         S   Africa

Asia

Japan

I live in the **Far East**.

South
America

Equator

Australia

Oceania

I rear sheep in
Australia which
is **South East**
the British Isle

Antarctica

Penguins are found only here in the **South**.

iew of four houses in a village
s. **2, 4, 6** and **8 West Road**.

A view of part of the village.
The arrow points to the four houses.

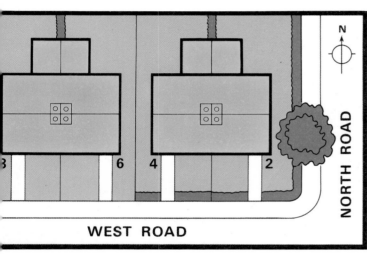

A plan of the four houses.
Scale: 1 cm to 3 m

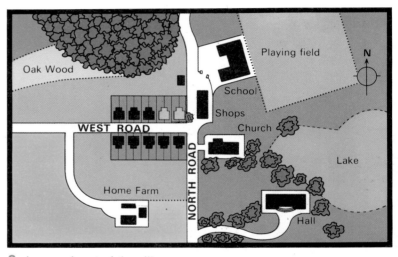

2 A map of part of the village.
Scale: 1 cm to 30 m

The rectangles **1** to **4** are all the same size.

1 and **2** are **large-scale maps**
showing **small** areas.
3 and **4** are **small-scale maps**
showing **large** areas.

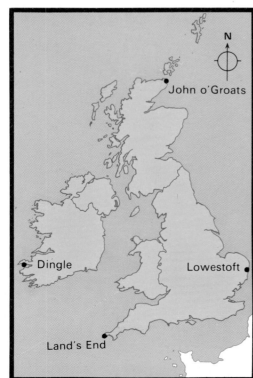

A map of the British Isles.
Scale: 1 cm to 125 km
The four places shown are
N, S, E and W on the mainland.

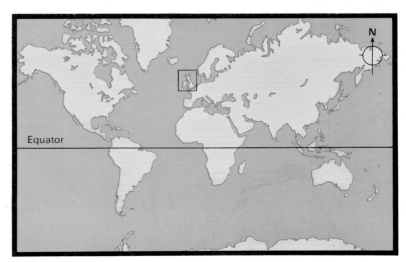

4 A map of the World.
Scale: 1 cm to 4200 km

British Isles

Highlands, lowlands, rivers and lakes

Highest mountain in each country

▲1 Ben Nevis 1343 m

▲2 Snowdon 1085 m

▲3 Carrauntoohill 1085 m

▲4 Scafell Pikes 978 m

▲5 Slieve Donard 852 m

Longest river in each country

River Shannon 386 km

River Severn 354 km

River Thames 346 km

River Tay 188 km

River Tywi 105 km

River Bann 96 km

Largest natural lake in each country

① Lough Neagh 382 km²

② Lough Corrib 176 km²

③ Loch Lomond 71 km²

④ Lake Windermere 14.7 km²

Countries and capitals – flags and population

England

England
47.7 million

London
6.76 million

Scotland

Scotland
5.1 million

Edinburgh
0.44 million

Republic of Ireland

Republic of Ireland 3.5 million

Dublin
0.51 million

Wales

Wales
2.9 million

Cardiff
0.28 million

Northern Ireland

Northern Ireland
1.6 million

Belfast
0.3 million

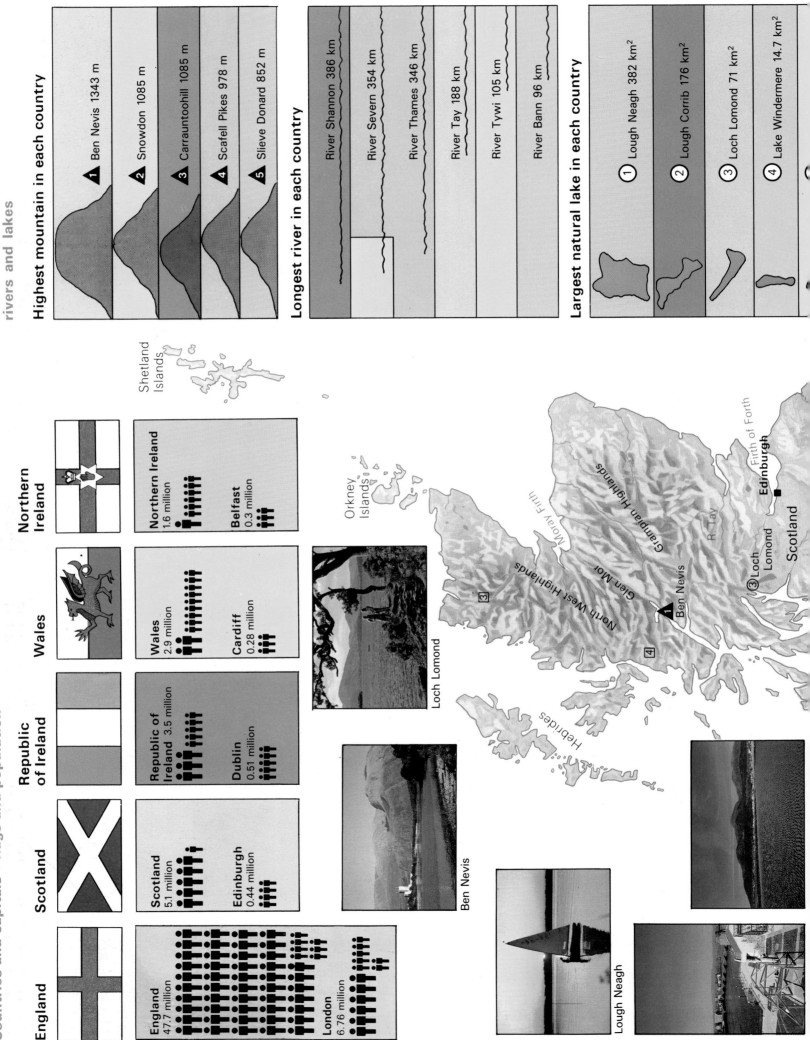

Shetland Islands

Orkney Islands

Moray Firth

Glen Mor

North West Highlands

Grampian Highlands

R. Tay

Firth of Forth

Edinburgh

Scotland

Ben Nevis

③ Loch Lomond

Hebrides

Loch Lomond

Ben Nevis

Lough Neagh

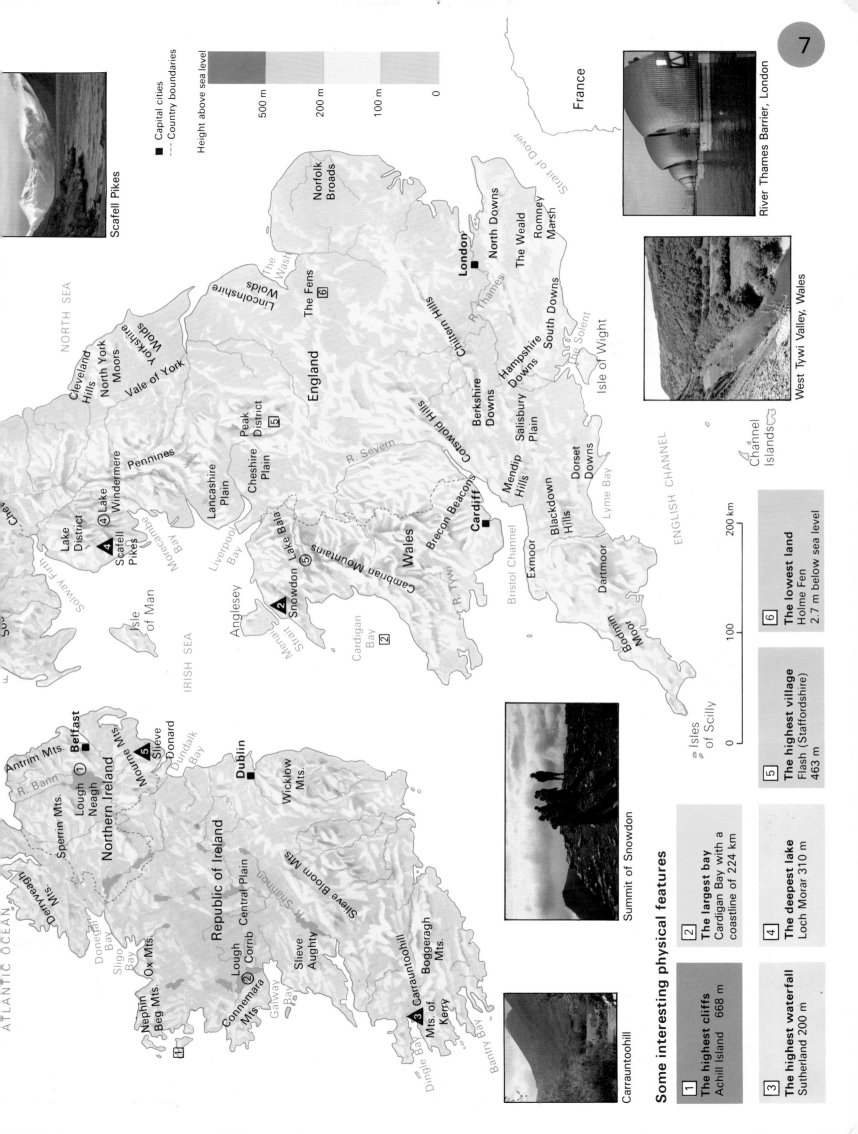

Key
- ■ Capital cities
- --- Country boundaries

Height above sea level
- 500 m
- 200 m
- 100 m
- 0

Scafell Pikes

River Thames Barrier, London

West Tywi Valley, Wales

Summit of Snowdon

Carrauntoohill

Some interesting physical features

1 The highest cliffs
Achill Island 668 m

2 The largest bay
Cardigan Bay with a coastline of 224 km

3 The highest waterfall
Sutherland 200 m

4 The deepest lake
Loch Morar 310 m

5 The highest village
Flash (Staffordshire) 463 m

6 The lowest land
Holme Fen 2.7 m below sea level

0   100   200 km

County boundaries, cities and towns

Top eight cities
Population (to nearest 10 000) ◎
Other cities, towns and administrative centres •

London pop. 6 760 000

Birmingham pop. 990 000

Leeds pop. 710 000

Sheffield pop. 530 000

Liverpool pop. 470 000

Bradford pop. 470 000

England
is divided into
Greater London
and 45 Counties.

In area **North Yorkshire**
is the largest County and
the **Isle of Wight** is the
smallest.

– – – – Country borders
. . . . . County boundaries

Manchester pop. 440 000

Bristol pop. 370 000

SCOTLAND

Berwick-on-Tweed

Northumberland

Morpeth •

Newcastle • Tyne
and Wear •

Carlisle •

Durham •
Durham

NORTH SEA

Cumbria

Stockton • • Middlesbrough
Cleveland

• Northallerton

North Yorkshire

• Ripon

Isle
of
Man
• Douglas

• Barrow

Morecambe Bay

York •

Beverley •

Humberside

Hull •

• Lancaster

Lancashire

Bradford ◎ ◎ **Leeds**

West
Yorkshire

Wakefield •

IRISH SEA

• Blackpool
Preston • Blackburn •

Greater
Manchester

South Yorkshire

Merseyside
Manchester ◎ **Sheffield** ◎

Liverpool ◎

Cheshire

Matlock •

Derbyshire

Nottingham •
Nottinghamshire

• Lincoln

Lincolnshire

• Chester

• Stoke

Boston •

The
Wash

• Stafford

Staffordshire

Derby •

Leicestershire

Norfolk

• Norwich

Shrewsbury •

Shropshire

• Leicester

Peterborough •

Cambridgeshire

Suffolk

WALES

West ◎ **Birmingham**
Midlands • Coventry •

Worcester • Warwick •
Warwickshire

Northamptonshire

Northampton •

Bedfordshire
• Bedford

Cambridge •

Ipswich •

Hereford
& Worcester

• Hereford

Luton •

Buckinghamshire

Hertfordshire

Hertford •

Essex

Chelmsford •

• Gloucester

Oxford •

Aylesbury •

Watford •

Southend •

Gloucestershire

Oxfordshire

London ◎

Bristol ◎

• Bath

Berkshire

Reading •

Canterbury •
Maidstone •

Avon

Wiltshire

Guildford •

Surrey

Kent

Trowbridge •

Hampshire

Bristol Channel

Somerset

Salisbury •

Winchester •

West Sussex

East Sussex

• Taunton

Southampton •

Lewes •

Chichester • Brighton •

Bournemouth

Portsmouth •

Devon

Dorset

• Newport
Isle of Wight

• Exeter

Dorchester •

0   30   60   90   120   15

Isles
of Scilly

Cornwall

• Plymouth

• Truro

Greater London
6 760 000

Areas of dense population, known as Metropolitans

West Midlands 2 617 000	Greater Manchester 2 578 000	West Yorkshire 2 057 000	Merseyside 1 448 000	South Yorkshire 1 293 000	Tyne and Wear 1 131 000

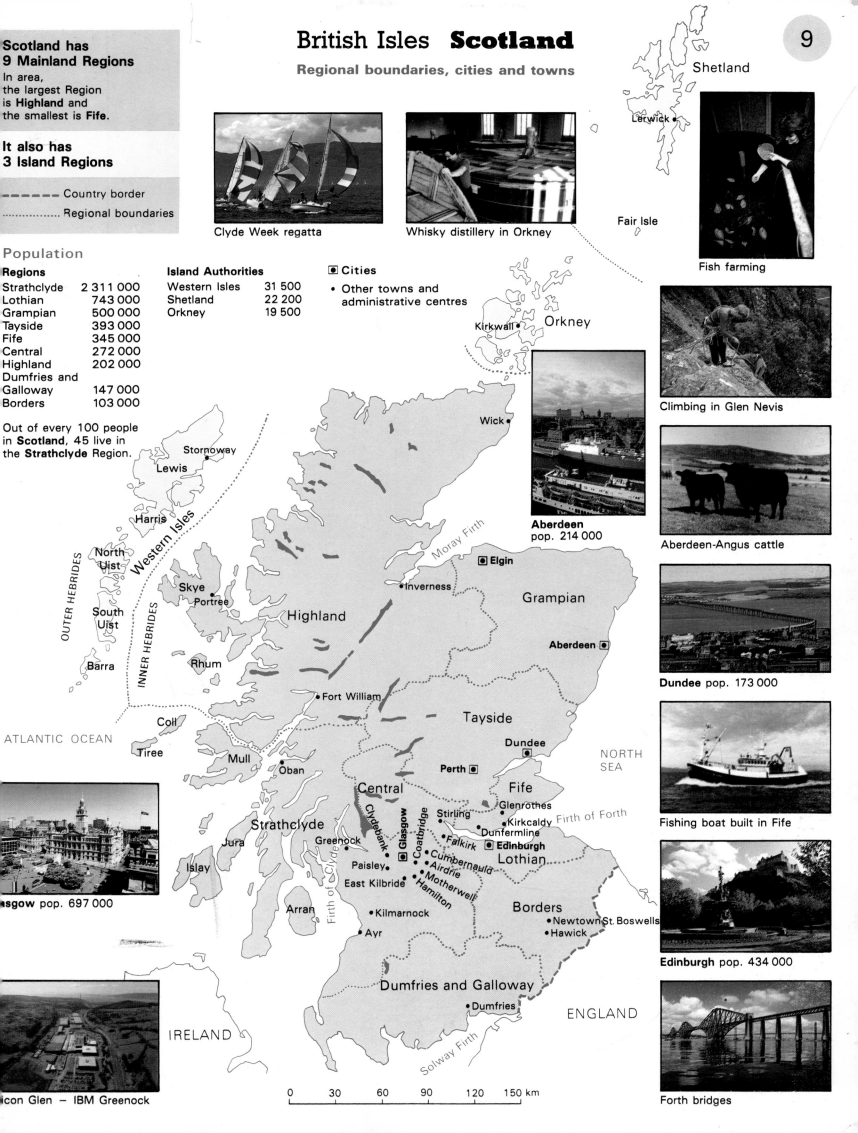

British Isles **Scotland**
Regional boundaries, cities and towns

Scotland has 9 Mainland Regions

In area, the largest Region is **Highland** and the smallest is **Fife**.

It also has 3 Island Regions

– – – – – Country border
.... Regional boundaries

Population

Regions	
Strathclyde	2 311 000
Lothian	743 000
Grampian	500 000
Tayside	393 000
Fife	345 000
Central	272 000
Highland	202 000
Dumfries and Galloway	147 000
Borders	103 000

Island Authorities	
Western Isles	31 500
Shetland	22 200
Orkney	19 500

Out of every 100 people in **Scotland**, 45 live in the **Strathclyde** Region.

⊡ Cities
• Other towns and administrative centres

Clyde Week regatta

Whisky distillery in Orkney

Shetland

Lerwick

Fair Isle

Fish farming

Climbing in Glen Nevis

Aberdeen-Angus cattle

Dundee pop. 173 000

Fishing boat built in Fife

Edinburgh pop. 434 000

Forth bridges

Aberdeen
pop. 214 000

Kirkwall • Orkney

Wick •

⊡ Elgin

• Inverness

Grampian

Highland

Aberdeen ⊡

Moray Firth

Stornoway

Lewis

Harris

North Uist

Skye
Portree

South Uist

Barra

OUTER HEBRIDES

Western Isles

INNER HEBRIDES

Rhum

Fort William •

Coll

Tiree

Mull

Oban •

ATLANTIC OCEAN

Tayside

Dundee
⊡

Perth ⊡

Central

Fife

Glenrothes

Stirling •

Kirkcaldy

Firth of Forth

Clydebank

Dunfermline

NORTH SEA

Strathclyde

Jura

Islay

Greenock

Paisley •

East Kilbride

⊡ Glasgow

Coatbridge

• Falkirk

⊡ Edinburgh

Cumbernauld

Airdrie

Motherwell •

Hamilton •

Lothian

Firth of Clyde

Arran

• Kilmarnock

• Ayr

Borders

• Newtown St. Boswells

• Hawick

Glasgow pop. 697 000

Dumfries and Galloway

• Dumfries

ENGLAND

IRELAND

Solway Firth

icon Glen – IBM Greenock

0   30   60   90   120   150 km

County boundaries, cities and towns

Wales
is divided into

**8 Counties
and 37 Districts**

In area
Dyfed is the largest County
and **South Glamorgan**
is the smallest.

– – – – – Country borders
.... County boundaries

Population of Counties

Mid Glamorgan	536 000
Gwent	445 000
Clwyd	407 000
South Glamorgan	403 000
West Glamorgan	363 000
Dyfed	348 000
Gwynedd	239 000
Powys	115 000

Out of every 100 people
in **Wales,** 62 live in the
South East within the 4
smallest Counties.

▣ **Cities**
• Large towns and
administrative centres

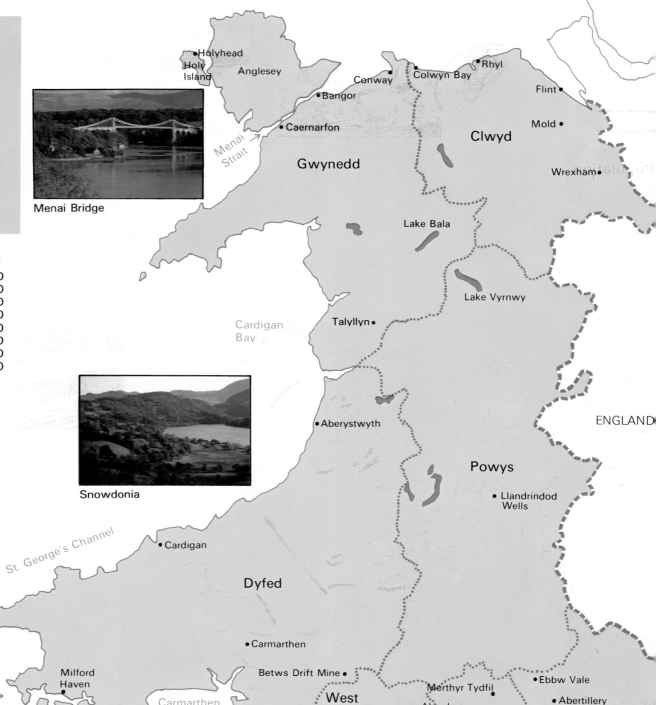

Menai Bridge

Snowdonia

Swansea pop. 187 000

Milford Haven refinery

Talyllyn narrow-gauge railway

Betws drift mine, South Wales

Welsh hill farm

Cardiff pop. 284 000

Eisteddfod

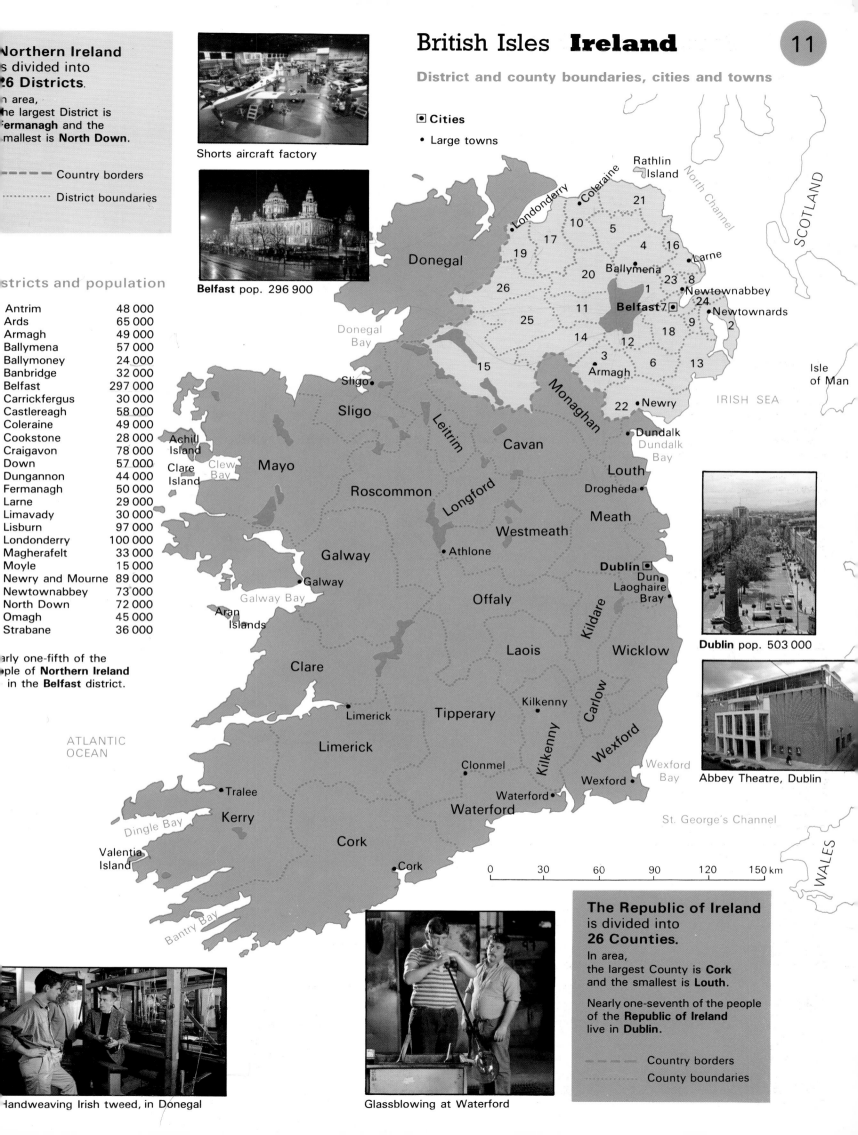

District and county boundaries, cities and towns

Northern Ireland is divided into 26 Districts.

In area, the largest District is **Fermanagh** and the smallest is **North Down.**

- – - – Country borders
- .... District boundaries

Shorts aircraft factory

Belfast pop. 296 900

⊡ Cities
• Large towns

Districts and population

Antrim	48 000
Ards	65 000
Armagh	49 000
Ballymena	57 000
Ballymoney	24 000
Banbridge	32 000
Belfast	297 000
Carrickfergus	30 000
Castlereagh	58 000
Coleraine	49 000
Cookstone	28 000
Craigavon	78 000
Down	57 000
Dungannon	44 000
Fermanagh	50 000
Larne	29 000
Limavady	30 000
Lisburn	97 000
Londonderry	100 000
Magherafelt	33 000
Moyle	15 000
Newry and Mourne	89 000
Newtownabbey	73 000
North Down	72 000
Omagh	45 000
Strabane	36 000

Nearly one-fifth of the people of **Northern Ireland** live in the **Belfast** district.

ATLANTIC OCEAN

Handweaving Irish tweed, in Donegal

Glassblowing at Waterford

Dublin pop. 503 000

Abbey Theatre, Dublin

The Republic of Ireland is divided into 26 Counties.

In area, the largest County is **Cork** and the smallest is **Louth.**

Nearly one-seventh of the people of the **Republic of Ireland** live in **Dublin.**

- – - – Country borders
- .... County boundaries

Harvest from the land

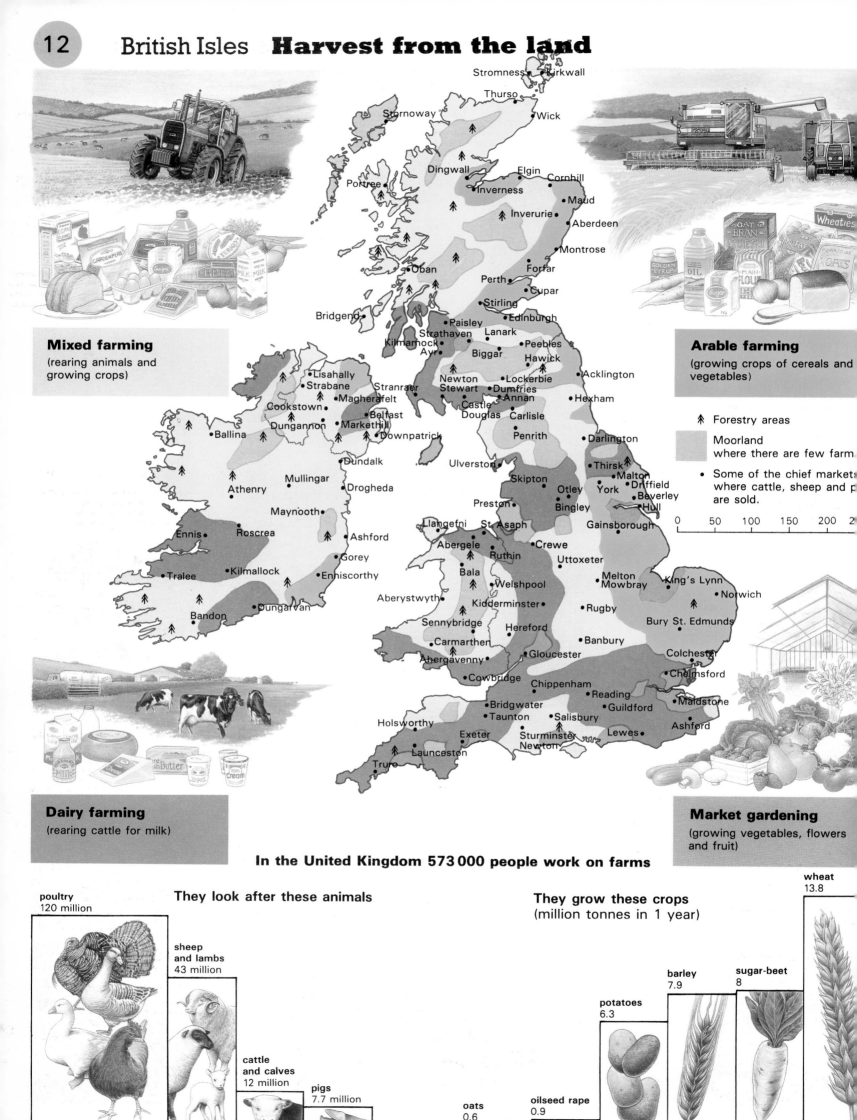

Mixed farming
(rearing animals and
growing crops)

Arable farming
(growing crops of cereals and
vegetables)

⍋ Forestry areas

Moorland
where there are few farm

• Some of the chief market
where cattle, sheep and p
are sold.

0   50   100   150   200

Dairy farming
(rearing cattle for milk)

Market gardening
(growing vegetables, flowers
and fruit)

Stromness • Kirkwall
Thurso
Stornoway   Wick
Dingwall   Elgin Cornhill
Portree   Inverness   Maud
Inverurie   Aberdeen
Montrose
Oban   Forfar
Perth   Cupar
Stirling
Bridgend   Edinburgh
Paisley   Lanark
Strathaven   Peebles
Kilmarnock   Biggar   Hawick
Ayr
Lisahally   Newton   Lockerbie   Acklington
Strabane   Stewart   Dumfries
Stranraer   Annan   Hexham
Cookstown   Magherafelt   Castle   Carlisle
Belfast   Douglas
Dungannon   Markethill   Penrith   Darlington
Ballina   Downpatrick
Ulverston   Thirsk
Dundalk   Malton
Skipton   Driffield
Athenry   Mullingar   Drogheda   Otley   York   Beverley
Preston   Bingley   Hull
Maynooth   Llangefni   St Asaph   Gainsborough
Abergele
Ennis   Roscrea   Ruthin   Crewe
Ashford   Bala   Uttoxeter
Gorey   Welshpool   Melton   King's Lynn
Tralee   Kilmallock   Enniscorthy   Mowbray   Norwich
Aberystwyth   Kidderminster   Rugby   Bury St. Edmunds
Bandon   Dungarvan   Sennybridge   Hereford
Carmarthen   Banbury   Colchester
Abergavenny   Gloucester   Chelmsford
Cowbridge   Maidstone
Chippenham   Reading
Bridgwater   Guildford   Ashford
Holsworthy   Taunton   Salisbury   Lewes
Exeter   Sturminster
Newton
Launceston
Truro

In the United Kingdom 573 000 people work on farms

They look after these animals

poultry
120 million

sheep
and lambs
43 million

cattle
and calves
12 million

pigs
7.7 million

They grow these crops
(million tonnes in 1 year)

wheat
13.8

barley
7.9

sugar-beet
8

potatoes
6.3

oats
0.6

oilseed rape
0.9

Types of fish brought into British ports showing percentage of each.
In one year the total catch weighs over 600 000 tonnes. It has fallen by nearly a half in the last twenty years.

On average each person in the British Isles eats nearly 8 kg of fish every year.

13% Shellfish

3.5% Plaice

6% Whiting

1% Skate

% Cod

HADDOCK

WHITING

COD

HERRING

MACKEREL

24% Mackerel

Principal fishing ports of the British Isles and location of some fishing grounds

HADDOCK

13% Haddock

Scalloway • Lerwick

AREAS OF FISH FARMING

Stornoway •

Kinlochbervie

SCAMPI

Ullapool

SCAMPI

MACKEREL

Mallaig

PLAICE

Scotland

Fraserburgh
Peterhead
Aberdeen

HADDOCK

WHITING

SHRIMPS

17% Other kinds of fish

WHITING

ATLANTIC OCEAN

SPRAT

HADDOCK

NORTH SEA

Halibut

5% Herring

HERRING

Killybegs •

Northern Ireland

Portavogie
Ardglass
Kilkeel

Whitehaven

SOLE

Seahouses
Amble
North Shields
Sunderland
Hartlepool
South Gare
Breakwater
Whitby
Scarborough
Bridlington
Hull
Grimsby

SPRAT

COD

WHITING

PLAICE

SOLE

Mullet

Sole

IRISH SEA

Fleetwood

Galway •

Howth

Republic of Ireland

SCAMPI

Caernarfon

Dunmore East

Castletown Bere

Milford Haven

Wales

England

King's Lynn

Lowestoft

Hake

Turbot

erman with lop lantern net

PLAICE

HERRING   SCAMPI   SOLE

0   60   120   180   240   300 km

Appledore
Bideford
Padstow
Plymouth Teignmouth
Mevagissey Looe Brixham
Newlyn Falmouth
MACKEREL   PLAICE

SOLE
Whitstable
Ramsgate
Folkestone
Newhaven Hastings

COD

OYSTERS

ENGLISH CHANNEL

Britain's fishing industry has
17 100 full-time fishermen
7859 inshore vessels
and 273 deep-sea vessels

w fish is caught

awling, for sea-bed fish

Purse seining, for surface fish

Creels and pots for shellfish

Fish farming employs about 5000 people. Farming of salmon and trout is already very successful. Production of shellfish, too, is increasing. The industry is making great efforts to develop farms for species of fish that are in short supply.

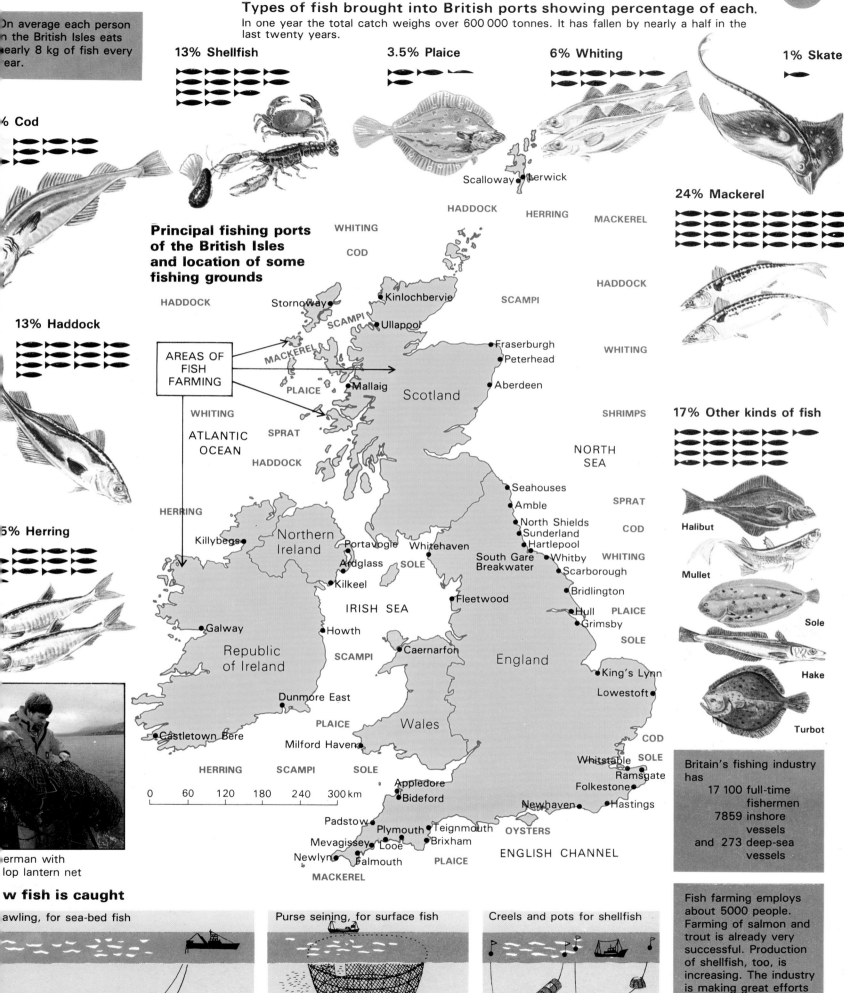

British Isles **People watching sport**

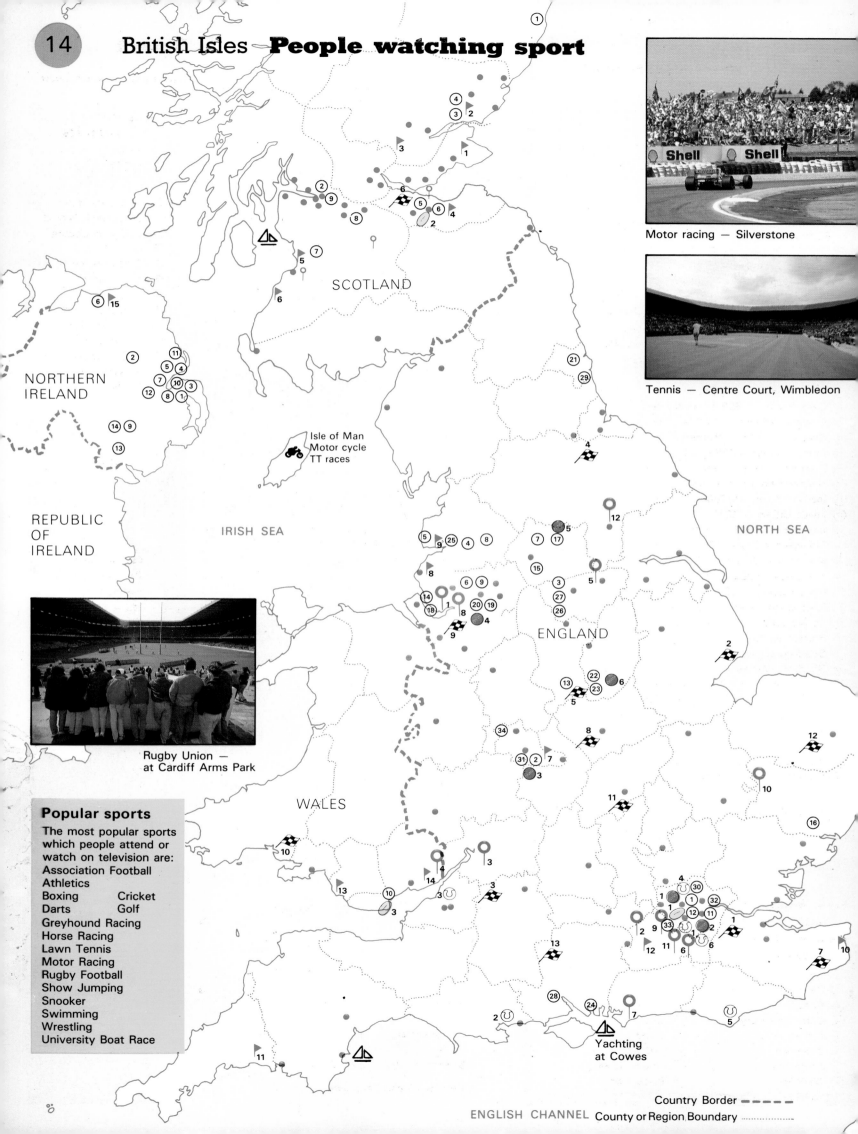

Motor racing — Silverstone

Tennis — Centre Court, Wimbledon

Rugby Union —
at Cardiff Arms Park

SCOTLAND

NORTHERN
IRELAND

REPUBLIC
OF
IRELAND

IRISH SEA

NORTH SEA

Isle of Man
Motor cycle
TT races

ENGLAND

WALES

Popular sports

The most popular sports
which people attend or
watch on television are:
Association Football
Athletics
Boxing   Cricket
Darts   Golf
Greyhound Racing
Horse Racing
Lawn Tennis
Motor Racing
Rugby Football
Show Jumping
Snooker
Swimming
Wrestling
University Boat Race

Yachting
at Cowes

ENGLISH CHANNEL

Country Border **– – – –**
County or Region Boundary ·············

Association Football

England  Wales

Some famous Clubs who have won the F.A. Cup or Football League
(showing Year Founded and Name of Ground)

1. Arsenal — 1886 — Highbury
2. Aston Villa — 1874 — Villa Park
3. Barnsley — 1887 — Oakwell Ground
4. Blackburn Rovers — 1875 — Ewood Park
5. Blackpool — 1887 — Bloomfield Road
6. Bolton Wanderers — 1874 — Burnden Park
7. Bradford City — 1903 — Valley Parade
8. Burnley — 1881 — Turf Moor
9. Bury — 1885 — Gigg Lane
10. Cardiff City — 1899 — Ninian Park
11. Charlton Athletic — 1905 — The Valley
12. Chelsea — 1905 — Stamford Bridge
13. Derby County — 1884 — Baseball Ground
14. Everton — 1878 — Goodison Park
15. Huddersfield Town — 1908 — Leeds Road
16. Ipswich Town — 1880 — Portman Road
17. Leeds United — 1919 — Elland Road
18. Liverpool — 1892 — Anfield
19. Manchester City — 1887 — Maine Road
20. Manchester United — 1880 — Old Trafford
21. Newcastle United — 1882 — St. James' Park
22. Notts County — 1862 — Meadow Lane
23. Nottingham Forest — 1865 — City Ground
24. Portsmouth — 1898 — Fratton Park
25. Preston North End — 1880 — Deepdale
26. Sheffield United — 1889 — Bramall Lane
27. Sheffield Wednesday — 1867 — Hillsborough
28. Southampton — 1885 — The Dell
29. Sunderland — 1879 — Roker Park
30. Tottenham Hotspur — 1882 — White Hart Lane
31. West Bromwich — 1879 — The Hawthorns
32. West Ham United — 1900 — Upton Park
33. Wimbledon — 1889 — Plough Lane
34. Wolverhampton Wanderers — 1877 — Molineux

● Location of other League Clubs

Northern Ireland

Some leading Clubs in Northern Ireland — members of the Irish League

1. Ards
2. Ballymena United
3. Bangor
4. Carrick Rangers
5. Cliftonville
6. Coleraine
7. Crusaders
8. Distillery
9. Glenavon
10. Glentoran
11. Larne
12. Linfield
13. Newry Town
14. Portadown

Scotland

Some famous Clubs who have won the Scottish F.A. Cup and Scottish League
(showing Year Founded and Name of Ground)

1. Aberdeen — 1903 — Pittodrie Park
2. Celtic — 1888 — Celtic Park
3. Dundee — 1893 — Dens Park
4. Dundee United — 1910 — Tannadice Park
5. Heart of Midlothian — 1875 — Tynecastle Park
6. Hibernian — 1875 — Easter Road Park
7. Kilmarnock — 1869 — Rugby Park
8. Motherwell — 1885 — Fir Park
9. Rangers — 1873 — Ibrox Stadium

● Location of other Scottish League Clubs

Cricket Test Match Grounds

1. Lords
2. The Oval
3. Edgbaston
4. Old Trafford
5. Headingley
6. Trent Bridge

Lawn Tennis Tournament Centres

1. Wimbledon
2. Bournemouth
3. Bristol
4. Wembley
5. Eastbourne
6. Queen's Club (London)

Rugby Union
International Grounds

1. Twickenham
2. Murrayfield
3. National Stadium (Cardiff Arms Park)

Horse Racing
Some famous Courses

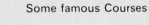

1. Aintree
2. Ascot
3. Cheltenham
4. Chepstow
5. Doncaster
6. Epsom
7. Goodwood
8. Haydock Park
9. Kempton Park
10. Newmarket
11. Sandown Park
12. York

Location of other Racecourses

Where people watch sport

Motor Racing Circuits

1. Brands Hatch
2. Cadwell Park
3. Castle Combe
4. Croft
5. Donington Park
6. Ingliston
7. Lydden
8. Mallory Park
9. Oulton Park
10. Pembrey
11. Silverstone
12. Snetterton
13. Thruxton

Golf
Championship courses

1. St. Andrews
2. Carnoustie
3. Gleneagles
4. Muirfield
5. Royal Troon
6. Turnberry
7. The Belfry
8. Royal Birkdale
9. Royal Lytham and St. Annes
10. Royal St. George's
11. St. Mellion
12. Wentworth
13. Royal Porthcawl
14. St. Pierre
15. Portrush

Marathons

Many cities and towns now have an annual marathon race of 26 miles (42 km). The most famous is the London Marathon.

Where they go

- 24% to West Country (incl. Scilly Isles)
- 12% to Scotland
- 12% to Wales
- 9% to Southern (incl. Isle of Wight)
- 8% to Yorkshire & Humberside
- 7% to East Anglia
- 7% to North West (incl. Isle of Man)
- 5% to South East
- 5% to East Midlands
- 4% to Heart of England (West Midlands)
- 4% to Cumbria
- 3% to Northumbria
- 2% to Thames & Chilterns
- 1% to Northern Ireland
- 1% to Greater London

(Percentages have been rounded)

National Trust Properties – Top 25

Total visitors in one year

1	Fountains Abbey & Studley	300 067
2	Stourhead Garden	228 399
3	St. Michael's Mount	194 973
4	Polesden Lacey	192 738
5	Styal, Quarry Bank Mill	187 841
6	Chartwell	181 983
7	Bodnant Garden	170 105
8	Sissinghurst	170 075
9	Wakehurst Place	168 541
10	Bodiam Castle	164 304
11	Corfe Castle	163 221
12	Lanhydrock	148 241
13	Tatton Park Garden	135 258
14	Housesteads Roman Fort	132 509
15	Sheffield Park Garden	125 248
16	Brownsea Island	124 269
17	Hidcote Manor Gardens	118 400
18	Castle Drogo	110 958
19	Cliveden	109 209
20	Kingston Lacy	108 552
21	Belton House	107 288
22	Killerton	105 828
23	Calke Abbey	105 753
24	Wimpole Home Farm	104 577
25	Blickling	103 355

Properties belonging to the National Trust for Scotland which have a total of approximately 100 000 visitors in one year include:

Brodick Castle, Brodie Castle, Culloden, Culzean Castle and Inverewe.

In Northern Ireland, Giant's Causeway has 350 000 visitors in one year.

Tourists from Britain and overseas spend £18 000 million on holidays in Britain each year. The jobs of 1.5 million people depend on tourism in Britain.

Beamish open air museum

Skiing in the Cairngorms

Walking in the Peak District

Where they stay

20% in a caravan

Tourist Attractions – Top 20

Total visitors in one year

1	Blackpool Pleasure Beach	6 500 000*

Shetland Islands

Lerwick

Orkney Islands

Stromness

Wick

Ullapool

Inverewe

Portree
Isle of Skye

Tobermory

Outer Hebrides

Brodie Castle
Culloden

Inverness

Cairngorms

Scotland

Glencoe

Oban

Inveraray

Dunoon

Rothesay

Brodick Castle

Ayr

Culzean Castle

Fraserburgh

Aberdeen

Crathes Castle

Blair

Scone

Doune

Stirling
Bannockburn

Culross

Strathclyde Country Park

Dundee

Dunbar

Edinburgh

NORTH SEA

Alnwick

Whitley Bay

Beamish

Northumberland National Park

Northumbria

Yorkshire Dales

Cumbria

Lake District

Morecambe

Isle of Man

Douglas

Whitby

North York Moors

Scarborough

Bridlington

Castle Howard

York

Yorkshire &

North

ATLANTIC OCEAN

Giant's Causeway

Portrush
Dunluce
Portstewart

Northern Ireland

Carrickfergus

Bangor

Ulster-American Folk Park

Castle Ward

Newcastle

Castle Coole

Florence Court

Sligo

km
0 40 80 120

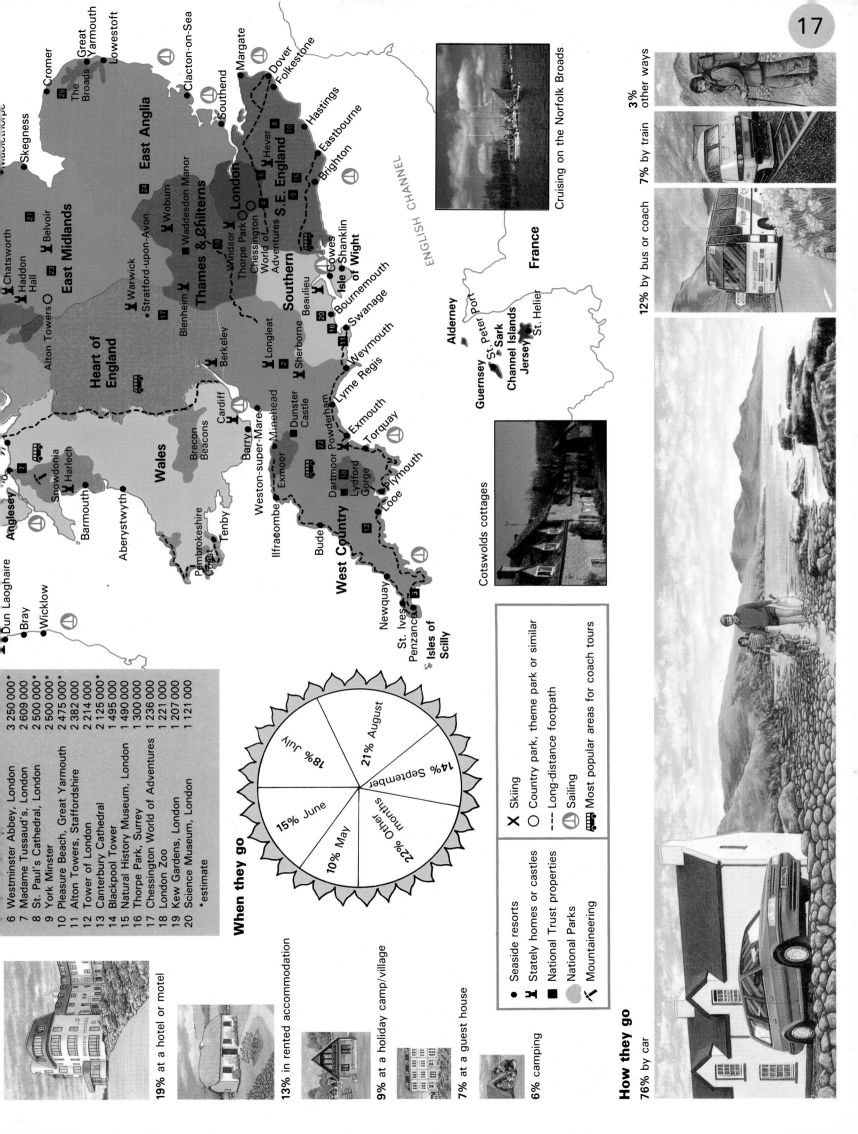

Map labels

Cromer, The Broads, Great Yarmouth, Lowestoft, Skegness, Clacton-on-Sea, Southend, Margate, Dover, Folkestone, Hastings, Eastbourne, Brighton

East Anglia

East Midlands — Chatsworth, Haddon Hall, Belvoir, Alton Towers, Warwick, Stratford-upon-Avon, Woburn, Waddesdon Manor

Thames & Chilterns — Blenheim, Windsor, Thorpe Park, Chessington World of Adventures, London

S.E. England — Hever

Heart of England — Berkeley, Longleat, Sherborne

Wales — Snowdonia, Harlech, Barmouth, Aberystwyth, Brecon Beacons, Cardiff, Barry, Tenby, Pembrokeshire Coast

Anglesey, Dun Laoghaire, Bray, Wicklow

Southern — Beaulieu, Cowes, Isle of Wight, Shanklin, Bournemouth, Swanage

West Country — Weston-super-Mare, Minehead, Ilfracombe, Dunster Castle, Exmoor, Dartmoor, Lydford Gorge, Powderham, Exmouth, Torquay, Weymouth, Lyme Regis, Plymouth, Looe, Bude, Newquay, St. Ives, Penzance, Isles of Scilly

ENGLISH CHANNEL

France — Alderney, Guernsey, St. Peter Port, Sark, St. Helier, Jersey, **Channel Islands**

Cruising on the Norfolk Broads

Cotswolds cottages

Attractions list

6	Westminster Abbey, London	3 250 000*
7	Madame Tussaud's, London	2 609 000
8	St. Paul's Cathedral, London	2 500 000*
9	York Minster	2 500 000*
10	Pleasure Beach, Great Yarmouth	2 475 000*
11	Alton Towers, Staffordshire	2 382 000
12	Tower of London	2 214 000
13	Canterbury Cathedral	2 125 000*
14	Blackpool Tower	1 495 000
15	Natural History Museum, London	1 490 000
16	Thorpe Park, Surrey	1 300 000
17	Chessington World of Adventures	1 236 000
18	London Zoo	1 221 000
19	Kew Gardens, London	1 207 000
20	Science Museum, London	1 121 000

*estimate

When they go

- 21% August
- 18% July
- 15% June
- 10% May
- 22% Other months
- 14% September

Legend

- ● Seaside resorts
- ♟ Stately homes or castles
- ■ National Trust properties
- National Parks
- Mountaineering
- ✗ Skiing
- ○ Country park, theme park or similar
- – – – Long-distance footpath
- Sailing
- Most popular areas for coach tours

How they go

76% by car

12% by bus or coach

7% by train

3% other ways

Accommodation

- 19% at a hotel or motel
- 13% in rented accommodation
- 9% at a holiday camp/village
- 7% at a guest house
- 6% camping

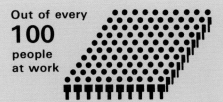

Out of every **100** people at work

In Britain there are nearly 29 million people available for work.

Of those in work, 44% are women.

In recent years the number of workers in manufacturing industries has fallen sharply to 5.2 million.

'Service' industries have shown a huge increase and they now employ nearly 16 million people. Services are required all over the country.

6 produce raw materials

20 make things

5 build things

69 serve other people

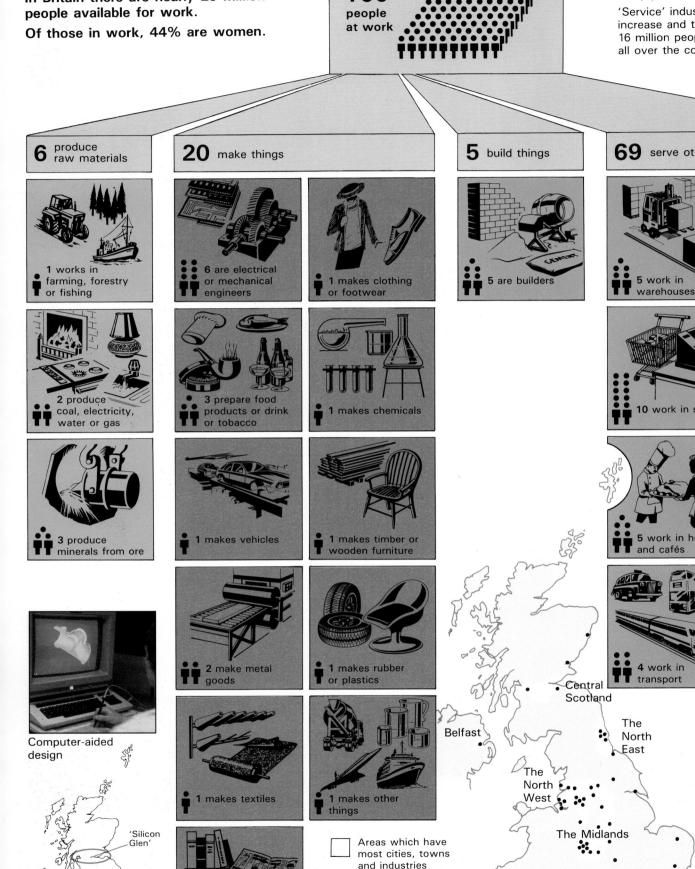

1 works in farming, forestry or fishing

6 are electrical or mechanical engineers

1 makes clothing or footwear

5 are builders

5 work in warehouses

2 work in postal services and communications

2 produce coal, electricity, water or gas

3 prepare food products or drink or tobacco

1 makes chemicals

10 work in shops

12 work in banks and insurance companies

3 produce minerals from ore

1 makes vehicles

1 makes timber or wooden furniture

5 work in hotels and cafés

7 work in local and national government

2 make metal goods

1 makes rubber or plastics

4 work in transport

8 work in education

Computer-aided design

1 makes textiles

1 makes other things

2 make paper or print books or newspapers

Areas which have most cities, towns and industries

• Large towns

'Silicon Glen'

'Silicon Fen' and M4 Corridor

Areas of high tech industry – software, semiconductors, robotics, biotechnology

0   100   200   300 km

Central Scotland

Belfast

The North East

The North West

The Midlands

London and the South East

S. Wales

Southampton/ Portsmouth area

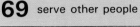
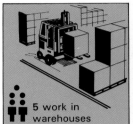

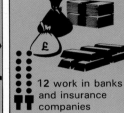

7 work in the Health Service

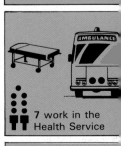

9 provide other services

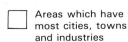

It is estimated that there is enough coal underground in the British Isles to last for more than 300 years.

What can be made from coal

Chemicals, detergents and perfume

Petrol, diesel and aircraft fuel

Tar, paint and printing ink

Fertilizers and garden sprays

Plastic and nylon

Gas and explosives

How coal is used

Electricity 82%

Industry 9%

Coke ovens 3%

Heating homes 3%

Other uses (including exports) 3%

British Coal – Coalfield Groups

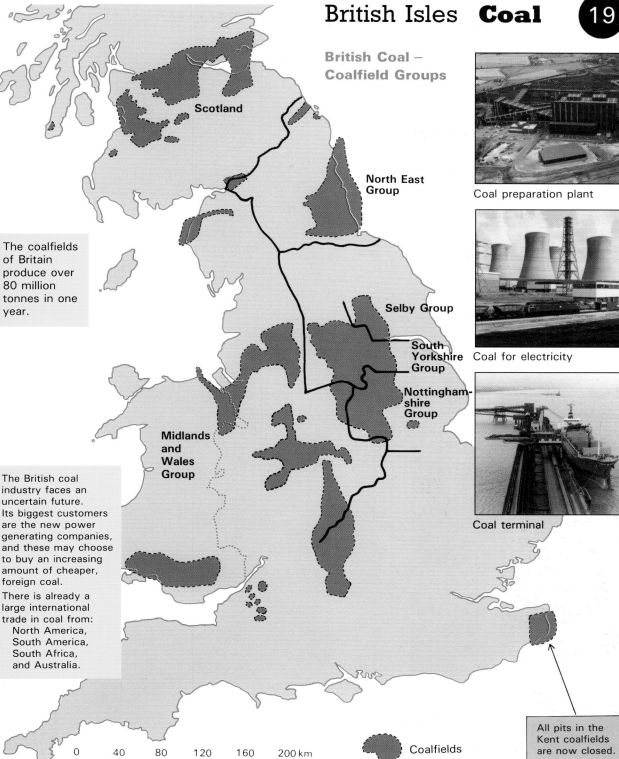

Scotland

North East Group

Selby Group

South Yorkshire Group

Nottinghamshire Group

Midlands and Wales Group

The coalfields of Britain produce over 80 million tonnes in one year.

The British coal industry faces an uncertain future. Its biggest customers are the new power generating companies, and these may choose to buy an increasing amount of cheaper, foreign coal.

There is already a large international trade in coal from: North America, South America, South Africa, and Australia.

0 40 80 120 160 200 km

Coalfields

All pits in the Kent coalfields are now closed.

Coal preparation plant

Coal for electricity

Coal terminal

ch colliery has at least two shafts or ts (sloping tunnels) leading from the face to the underground workings. The rage depth is 350 m and the average ckness of the seam of coal is 1.6 m. ne pits have over 35 km of derground roads.

British Coal employs about 74 000 people.
Of these more than three-quarters are miners and about one-third of these work at the coal-face.

Machines called power loaders cut the coal. They automatically load the coal onto conveyors for the journey out of the mine. An increasing number of power loaders are being fitted with sensing devices which automatically steer them along the coal seam. Hydraulic roof supports protect miners at the coal face.

Opencast mining takes place on the surface and adds about 17 million tonnes a year to the output from underground mines. A giant drag-line, 'Big Geordie' operating in Northumberland, weighs more than 2800 tonnes and its bucket carries 50 cubic metres – equivalent to about nine 'Mini' cars.

ow al is rried

80% by rail

14% by road

6% by water or conveyors direct from some pits to adjacent power stations

What Natural Gas is used for

Glassworks
Pottery industry
Iron and steel
processes
Factories
Offices
Shops
Power stations
(700 000
customers)

In industry and commerce (47%)

Central heating

Cookers

Fires

Water
heaters

In the home (53%) 17 million customers

A processing platform

A shore terminal

Laying the pipe

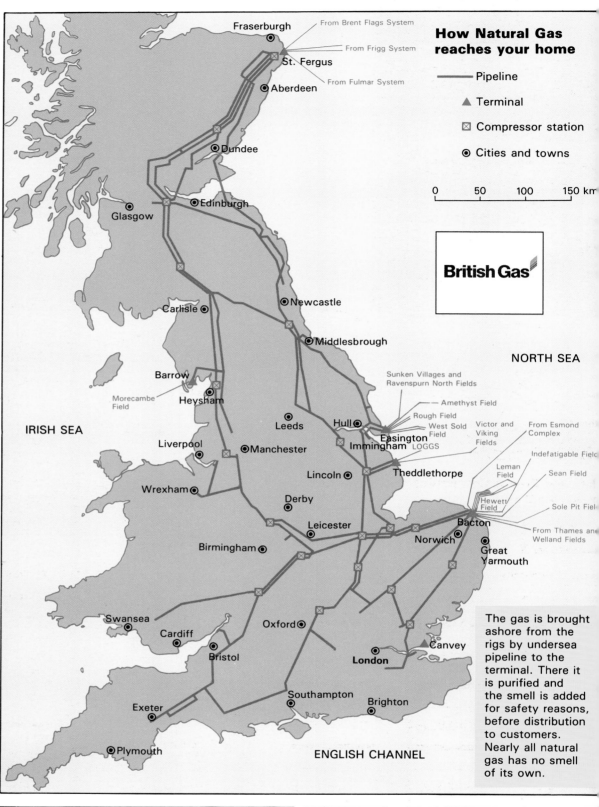

How Natural Gas reaches your home

— Pipeline
▲ Terminal
⊠ Compressor station
⊙ Cities and towns

0   50   100   150 km

British Gas

Fraserburgh
From Brent Flags System
From Frigg System
St. Fergus
From Fulmar System
Aberdeen

Dundee

Glasgow
Edinburgh

NORTH SEA

Carlisle
Newcastle

Middlesbrough

Sunken Villages and
Ravenspurn North Fields

Barrow
Morecambe
Field
Heysham

Amethyst Field
Rough Field
West Sold
Field
Victor and
Viking
Fields
From Esmond
Complex

Leeds
Hull

Liverpool
Manchester
Easington
Immingham   LOGGS

Indefatigable Field

Theddlethorpe
Leman
Field
Sean Field

Lincoln

Wrexham
Derby

Hewett
Field
Sole Pit Field

IRISH SEA

Leicester
Bacton

Birmingham
Norwich
Great
Yarmouth

From Thames and
Welland Fields

Swansea
Oxford
Canvey

Cardiff
London

Bristol

The gas is brought
ashore from the
rigs by undersea
pipeline to the
terminal. There it
is purified and
the smell is added
for safety reasons,
before distribution
to customers.
Nearly all natural
gas has no smell
of its own.

Exeter
Southampton
Brighton

Plymouth

ENGLISH CHANNEL

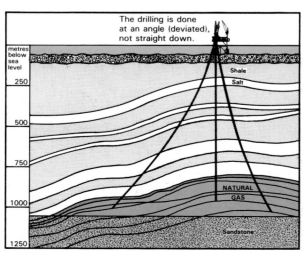

The drilling is done
at an angle (deviated),
not straight down.

metres
below
sea
level

Shale
Salt

250

500

750

NATURAL
GAS

1000

Sandstone

1250

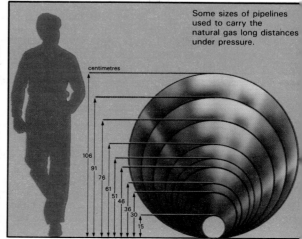

Some sizes of pipelines
used to carry the
natural gas long distances
under pressure.

centimetres

106
91
76
61
51
46
36
30
15

ow we use electricity

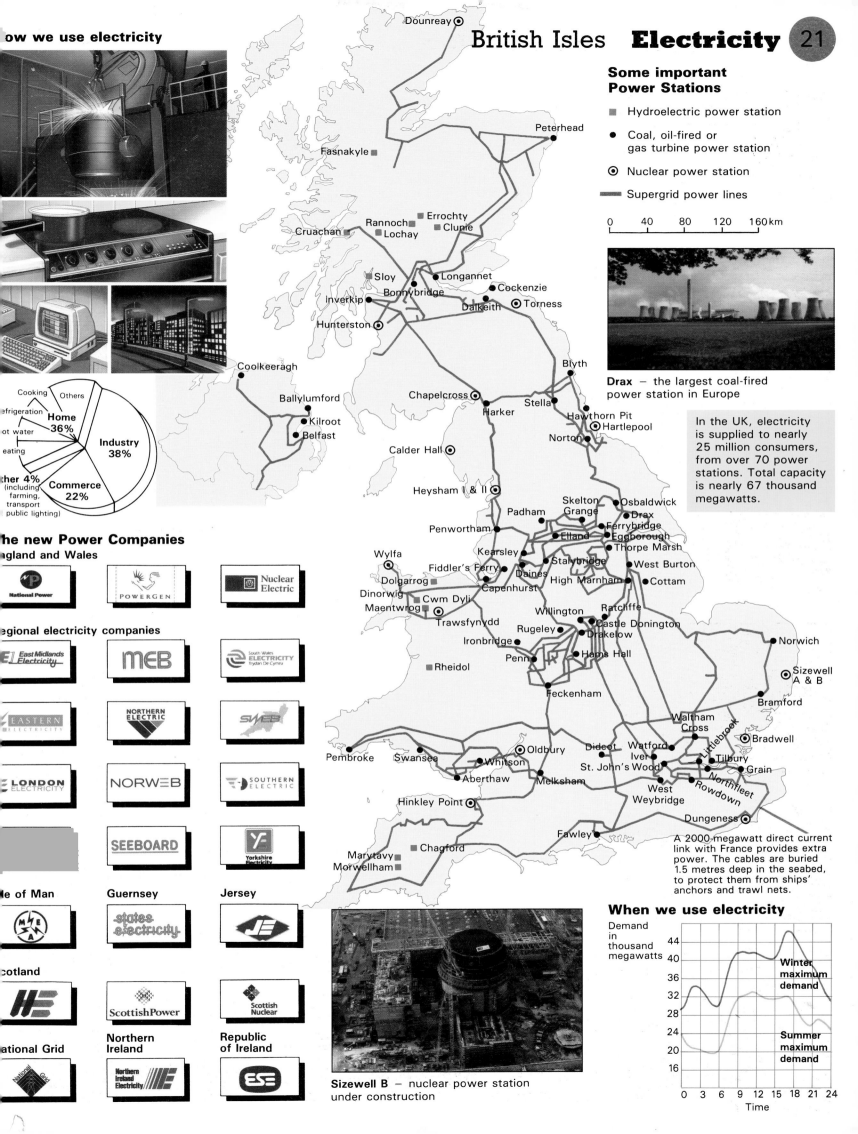

Some important Power Stations

- ■ Hydroelectric power station
- ● Coal, oil-fired or gas turbine power station
- ◉ Nuclear power station
- ▬ Supergrid power lines

```
0    40   80   120   160km
```

Drax — the largest coal-fired power station in Europe

In the UK, electricity is supplied to nearly 25 million consumers, from over 70 power stations. Total capacity is nearly 67 thousand megawatts.

Home 36%
Cooking, Others, efrigeration, ot water, eating

Industry 38%

her 4% (including farming, transport public lighting)

Commerce 22%

he new Power Companies

gland and Wales

National Power

POWERGEN

Nuclear Electric

egional electricity companies

East Midlands Electricity

MEB

South Wales ELECTRICITY Trydan De Cymru

EASTERN ELECTRICITY

NORTHERN ELECTRIC

SWEB

LONDON ELECTRICITY

NORWEB

SOUTHERN ELECTRIC

SEEBOARD

Yorkshire Electricity

le of Man

MEA

Guernsey

states electricity

Jersey

JE

cotland

HE

ScottishPower

Scottish Nuclear

ational Grid

National Grid

Northern Ireland

Northern Ireland Electricity

Republic of Ireland

ESB

Sizewell B — nuclear power station under construction

A 2000-megawatt direct current link with France provides extra power. The cables are buried 1.5 metres deep in the seabed, to protect them from ships' anchors and trawl nets.

When we use electricity

Demand in thousand megawatts

Winter maximum demand

Summer maximum demand

```
44
40
36
32
28
24
20
16
   0  3  6  9  12 15 18 21 24
              Time
```

Map labels: Dounreay, Peterhead, Fasnakyle, Errochty, Clunie, Rannoch, Lochay, Cruachan, Sloy, Longannet, Cockenzie, Bonnybridge, Dalkeith, Torness, Inverkip, Hunterston, Coolkeeragh, Blyth, Ballylumford, Chapelcross, Stella, Kilroot, Harker, Hawthorn Pit, Belfast, Norton, Hartlepool, Calder Hall, Heysham I & II, Skelton Grange, Osbaldwick, Padham, Drax, Penwortham, Ferrybridge, Elland, Eggborough, Thorpe Marsh, Kearsley, Stalybridge, West Burton, Wylfa, Fiddler's Ferry, Daines, Dolgarrog, Capenhurst, High Marnham, Cottam, Dinorwig, Cwm Dyli, Maentwrog, Willington, Ratcliffe, Trawsfynydd, Rugeley, Castle Donington, Ironbridge, Drakelow, Norwich, Penn, Hams Hall, Rheidol, Sizewell A & B, Feckenham, Bramford, Waltham Cross, Littlebrook, Bradwell, Pembroke, Swansea, Oldbury, Didcot, Watford, Iver, Tilbury, Whitson, St. John's Wood, Northfleet, Grain, Aberthaw, Melksham, West Weybridge, Rowdown, Hinkley Point, Dungeness, Fawley, Chagford, Marytavy, Morwellham

Weather in winter

Average temperatures (January)

Coldest
in the North

①

Mild
in the West

Cool
in the East

②

- 7°C - 8°C
- 6°C - 7°C
- 4°C - 6°C
- 3°C - 4°C
- less than 3°C

① Lowest temperature ever recorded, −27.2°C, at Braemar, 1895

② Longest freeze, 40 days below 0°C, Great Dun Fell, 1986

Average daily hours of sunshine (January)

Least sunshine
in the North

hours
- more than 2
- 2
- 1 - 1.5
- less than 1

Sunniest
in the South

Snowfall
Average number of days in a year when snow is on the ground

Most snow
in the North
and on mountains

②

①

days
- more than 100
- 30 - 100
- 10 - 30
- 5 - 10
- 0 - 5

Greatest snowfall in one year, 1520 mm, 1947, in
① Clwyd
② Upper Teesdale

Weather in summer

Average temperatures (July)

Coolest
in the North

①

- more than 17°C
- 16°C-17°C
- 14°C-16°C   **③**
- 13°C-14°C   **②**
- 12°C-13°C

Warmest
in the South

Highest temperature, 38.1°C, at
① Tonbridge, 1868

Hottest places throughout the year, 11.5°C average
② Penzance
③ Scilly Isles

Average daily hours of sunshine (July)

Least sunshine
in the North

①②

hours
- 7
- 6.5 - 7
- 6 - 6.5
- 5.5 - 6
- 5 - 5.5
- 4.5 - 5
- 4

Most sunshine
in the South

Most sunshine in one month, 384 hours, 1911, at
① Eastbourne
② Hastings

Rainfall and winds
Average total rainfall in one year

Wettest
in the West

Driest
in the East

④

①

②

③

mm
- over 1500
- 1000 - 1500
- 750 - 1000
- 625 - 750
- under 625

Most winds blow
from the
South West

Wettest place, 6528 mm annual average total, at
① Styhead Tarn, 1954

Driest place, 513 mm annual average total, at
② St. Osyth

Most rain in one day, 279.4 mm, at
③ Martinstown, 1955

Highest wind speed, 278.6 km/h, on
④ Cairn Gorm, 1986

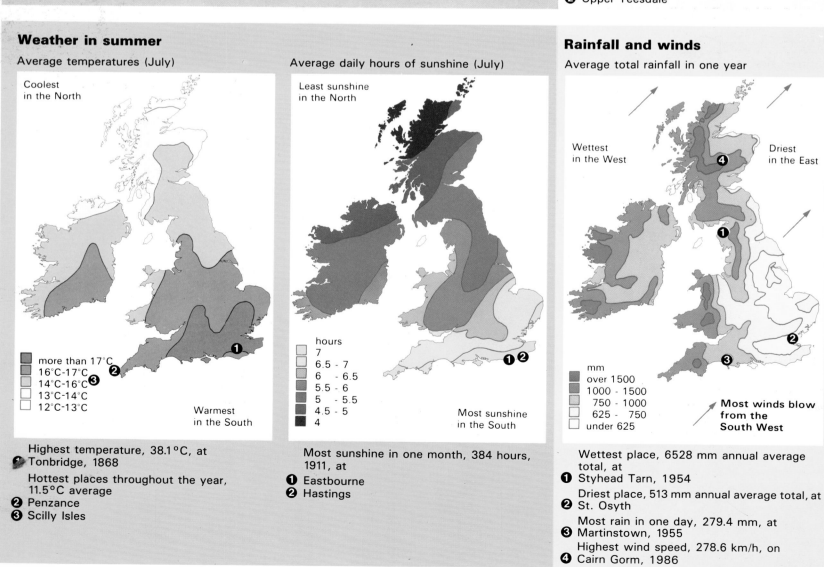

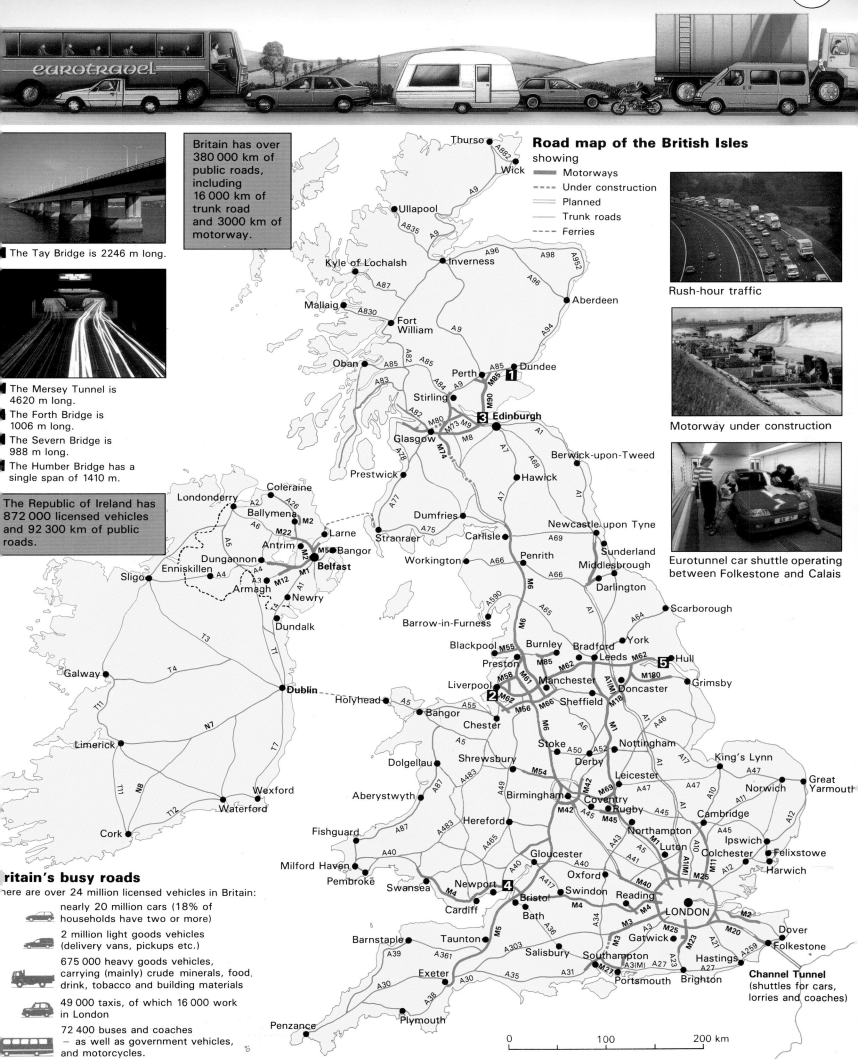

The Tay Bridge is 2246 m long.

The Mersey Tunnel is 4620 m long.

The Forth Bridge is 1006 m long.

The Severn Bridge is 988 m long.

The Humber Bridge has a single span of 1410 m.

Britain has over 380 000 km of public roads, including 16 000 km of trunk road and 3000 km of motorway.

The Republic of Ireland has 872 000 licensed vehicles and 92 300 km of public roads.

Road map of the British Isles
showing
- ▬▬ Motorways
- ---- Under construction
- ═══ Planned
- ─── Trunk roads
- ---- Ferries

Rush-hour traffic

Motorway under construction

Eurotunnel car shuttle operating between Folkestone and Calais

Britain's busy roads
There are over 24 million licensed vehicles in Britain:

- nearly 20 million cars (18% of households have two or more)
- 2 million light goods vehicles (delivery vans, pickups etc.)
- 675 000 heavy goods vehicles, carrying (mainly) crude minerals, food, drink, tobacco and building materials
- 49 000 taxis, of which 16 000 work in London
- 72 400 buses and coaches – as well as government vehicles, and motorcycles.

Transport by rail

British trains

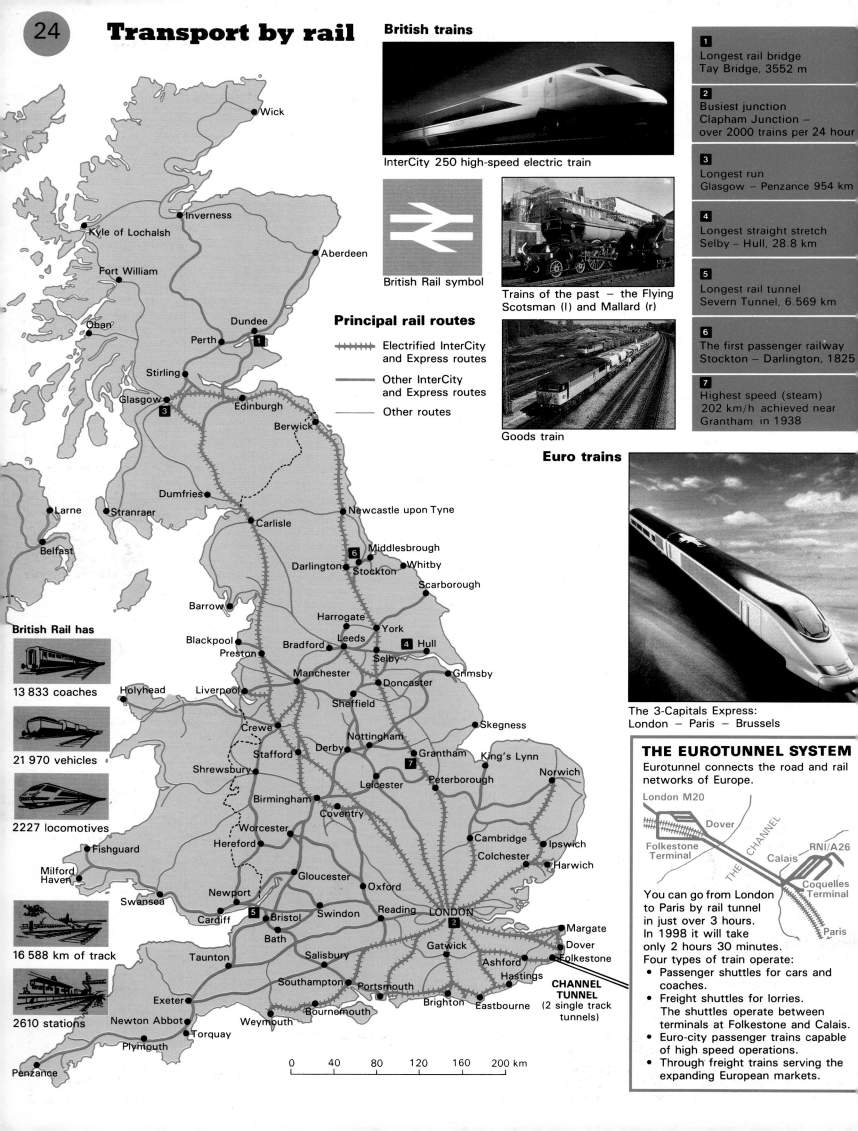

InterCity 250 high-speed electric train

British Rail symbol

Trains of the past – the Flying Scotsman (l) and Mallard (r)

Goods train

Principal rail routes

+++++ Electrified InterCity and Express routes

──── Other InterCity and Express routes

──── Other routes

1 Longest rail bridge
Tay Bridge, 3552 m

2 Busiest junction
Clapham Junction –
over 2000 trains per 24 hour

3 Longest run
Glasgow – Penzance 954 km

4 Longest straight stretch
Selby – Hull, 28.8 km

5 Longest rail tunnel
Severn Tunnel, 6.569 km

6 The first passenger railway
Stockton – Darlington, 1825

7 Highest speed (steam)
202 km/h achieved near
Grantham in 1938

Euro trains

The 3-Capitals Express:
London – Paris – Brussels

THE EUROTUNNEL SYSTEM

Eurotunnel connects the road and rail networks of Europe.

London M20

Dover

Folkestone Terminal

THE CHANNEL

Calais

RNI/A26

Coquelles Terminal

Paris

You can go from London to Paris by rail tunnel in just over 3 hours. In 1998 it will take only 2 hours 30 minutes.
Four types of train operate:
- Passenger shuttles for cars and coaches.
- Freight shuttles for lorries. The shuttles operate between terminals at Folkestone and Calais.
- Euro-city passenger trains capable of high speed operations.
- Through freight trains serving the expanding European markets.

British Rail has

13 833 coaches

21 970 vehicles

2227 locomotives

16 588 km of track

2610 stations

CHANNEL
TUNNEL
(2 single track
tunnels)

Map locations:
Wick, Kyle of Lochalsh, Inverness, Aberdeen, Fort William, Oban, Dundee, Perth, Stirling, Glasgow, Edinburgh, Berwick, Dumfries, Larne, Stranraer, Carlisle, Belfast, Newcastle upon Tyne, Middlesbrough, Darlington, Stockton, Whitby, Scarborough, Barrow, Harrogate, York, Blackpool, Bradford, Leeds, Hull, Preston, Selby, Manchester, Grimsby, Holyhead, Liverpool, Doncaster, Sheffield, Crewe, Skegness, Nottingham, Derby, Stafford, Grantham, King's Lynn, Shrewsbury, Leicester, Peterborough, Norwich, Birmingham, Coventry, Worcester, Cambridge, Ipswich, Hereford, Colchester, Harwich, Fishguard, Gloucester, Milford Haven, Oxford, Newport, Swindon, Reading, LONDON, Margate, Swansea, Cardiff, Bristol, Dover, Folkestone, Bath, Gatwick, Taunton, Salisbury, Ashford, Hastings, Southampton, Portsmouth, Brighton, Eastbourne, Exeter, Newton Abbot, Weymouth, Bournemouth, Torquay, Plymouth, Penzance

0 40 80 120 160 200 km

In the British Isles there are 151 airports or aerodromes, of which 46 are available for use by civil aircraft.

England and Wales	106
Scotland	37
Northern Ireland	4
Isle of Man	1
Channel Islands	3

There are a further 20 in the Republic of Ireland.

Boeing 737

British Aerospace ATP

Civil airlines

Top ten busiest airports in millions of passengers per year.

Heathrow	39.8
Gatwick	21.2
Manchester	10.1
Dublin	5.1
Glasgow	3.9
Birmingham	3.3
Luton	2.8
Edinburgh	2.4
Belfast	2.2
Aberdeen	1.7

Top five busiest airports in thousands of tonnes of cargo per year.

Heathrow	695
Gatwick	220
Manchester	72
Stansted	32
Belfast	24

Helicopters

There are over 40 commercial helicopter operators in the British Isles. Much of their work is ferrying crews and equipment to the North Sea oil and gas rigs. They are also involved in:

powerline construction
loading and unloading ships
dispersing oil slicks
salvage
fire-fighting

Aerospatiale AS 332L Super Puma

ATLANTIC OCEAN

NORTH SEA

IRISH SEA

ENGLISH CHANNEL

France

Shetland Islands
Lerwick

Orkney Islands
Kirkwall
Wick
Stornoway
To N. America
To N. America
Benbecula
Inverness
Aberdeen
Dundee
To N. America
Glasgow
Edinburgh
Prestwick
Newcastle
To N. America
Belfast
Teeside
Isle of Man
Ronaldsway
Leeds/Bradford
Blackpool
To N. America
Liverpool
Manchester
Dublin
Shannon
Norwich
East Midlands
Birmingham
Coventry
Cambridge
Ipswich
To Scandinavia
Cork
To N. America
Gloucester
Luton
Stansted
Swansea
Heathrow
Southend
To N. Europe
Cardiff
Bristol
Gatwick
Ashford
To N. America (Concorde route)
Southampton
Lydd
Exeter
Bournemouth
Portsmouth
To Europe
Isles of Scilly
Penzance
St. Mary's
Alderney
Guernsey
Channel Islands
Jersey

0 40 80 120 160 200 km

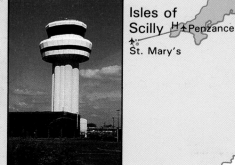
Control tower, Gatwick

...ssengers in aircraft

...ading cargo

✈	Airport
⊕	Major international airport
—	Air route
H	Heliport Helicopter operator

Denmark Tivoli, Copenhagen

Russia Kremlin, Moscow

Germany Brandenburg Gate, Berlin

France Versailles near Paris

Switzerland Ski resort

Austria Elmau, Tyrol

Norway Fiord cruising

Motorail through France

Eurotunnel

Unlike existing ferry services, the Channel Tunnel offers a free-flow system. Cars can turn up at any time without having to book. The tunnel is expected to have a major effect on the way people travel to mainland Europe.

How people leave the British Isles

Aircraft **73%**

Ship **26%**

Hovercraft **1%**

Finland

Estonia

Latvia

Lithuania

BALTIC SEA

Poland

• Warsaw ■

Romania

Czechoslovakia
✈ Prague

Hungary
■ Budapest

Vienna ✈■
Austria
• Graz
✈ Salzburg
• Bled
• Ljubljana
• Trieste

500 km
400
300
200
100
0

• Mora

Sweden
✈■ Stockholm
• Mariestad

✈ Göthenburg

Norway
✈ Oslo

• Sognefjord
• Bergen
• Haugesund
• Stavanger

• Aarhus
Denmark
■ Copenhagen
• Odense
• Esbjerg

• Hamburg
• Bremerhaven
✈ Hanover

Berlin ■✈
• Dresden
• Leipzig

Germany
✈ Frankfurt
• Heidelberg

Black Forest
• Freiburg

• Zurich
• Lucerne
Switzerland
• Berne
• Interlaken
Lake Maggiore
• Basel
• Geneva

• Munich ✈
• Innsbruck ✈
Tyrol

Italy
Lido di Jesolo

NORTH SEA

Netherlands
■ Amsterdam
• Hook of Holland
• Rotterdam

Belgium
■ Brussels
• Zeebrugge
• Ostend
• Dunkirk ✈
• Calais
• Boulogne
• Vlissingen
Eurotunnel
• Le Touquet

Luxem-bourg ■

• Cologne
• Bonn

• Nancy
• Strasbourg

✈ Edinburgh

✈ Glasgow

• Stranraer
• Newcastle ✈

• Leeds ✈
• Manchester ✈

• Hull

✈ Birmingham
East Midlands ✈

• Luton ✈
• Harwich
• Felixstowe
• Ramsgate
• Sheerness
London ■✈
✈ Dover
Newhaven
• Folkestone

• Bristol
• Southampton ✈
• Portsmouth
• Poole

• Reims
Paris ■✈

• Orleans

France

• Dieppe
• Le Havre
• Honfleur
• Deauville
• Cherbourg
• Caen
• St. Malo
• Dinard

Channel Islands
Côte d'Emeraude
• Roscoff
• Brest
Brittany
• St. Nazaire
• La Baule

Côte de...

• Glasgow
IRISH SEA
• Douglas
• Holyhead
• Fishguard ✈
• Swansea ✈
• Plymouth

• Larne
Belfast ■✈

Dublin ■✈
• Dun Laoghaire
• Rosslare
• Cork ✈

Key:
■ Capital City
• Resort, holiday centre
○ Seaport
— Car ferry route
✈ Airport
— Motorail route with destination

← Canada

← USA

Aircraft

Car ferry

Hovercraft/Hydrofoil

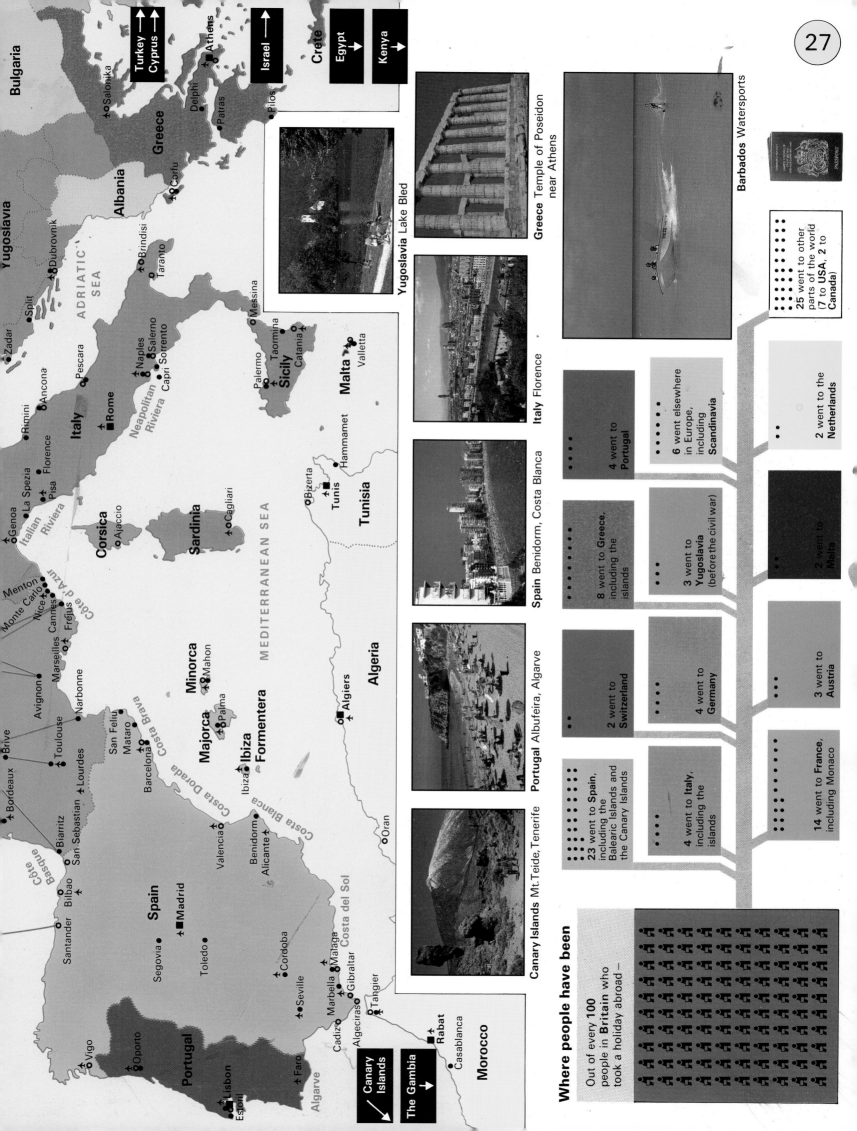

Bulgaria

Turkey →
Cyprus →

Israel →

Crete

Egypt →

Kenya →

Salonika
Delphi
Athens

Greece

Patras
Pilos

Corfu

Albania

Yugoslavia

Dubrovnik

Zadar
Split

ADRIATIC SEA

Brindisi
Taranto

Messina
Taormina
Catania

Palermo

Sicily

Valletta

Malta

Ancona
Pescara

Naples
Salerno Sorrento
Neapolitan Riviera Capri

Rome

Italy

Rimini
La Spezia
Florence
Pisa

Genoa
Italian Riviera

Corsica
Ajaccio

Cagliari

Sardinia

MEDITERRANEAN SEA

Bizerta
Tunis

Tunisia

Hammamet

Algiers

Algeria

Oran

Menton
Monte Carlo
Nice
Cannes
Fréjus

Côte d'Azur

Marseilles
Avignon
Narbonne

Brive
Bordeaux
Toulouse
Lourdes
Biarritz
San Sebastian

Côte Basque

Bilbao
Santander

San Feliu
Mataro
Barcelona

Costa Brava

Costa Dorada

Minorca
Mahon

Majorca
Palma

Ibiza
Formentera

Valencia

Benidorm
Alicante

Costa Blanca

Spain
Madrid

Segovia
Toledo

Cordoba
Seville

Marbella
Malaga
Gibraltar
Costa del Sol
Tangier

Cadiz
Algeciras

Rabat
Casablanca

Morocco

Canary Islands
The Gambia

Vigo
Oporto

Portugal
Lisbon
Estoril
Faro

Algarve

Yugoslavia Lake Bled

Greece Temple of Poseidon near Athens

Barbados Watersports

Italy Florence

Spain Benidorm, Costa Blanca

Portugal Albufeira, Algarve

Canary Islands Mt. Teide, Tenerife

Where people have been

Out of every 100 people in Britain who took a holiday abroad –

23 went to Spain, including the Balearic Islands and the Canary Islands

8 went to Greece, including the islands

4 went to Portugal

6 went elsewhere in Europe, including Scandinavia

25 went to other parts of the world (7 to USA, 2 to Canada)

2 went to Switzerland

3 went to Yugoslavia (before the civil war)

2 went to the Netherlands

4 went to Italy, including the islands

4 went to Germany

2 went to Malta

14 went to France, including Monaco

3 went to Austria

European Community

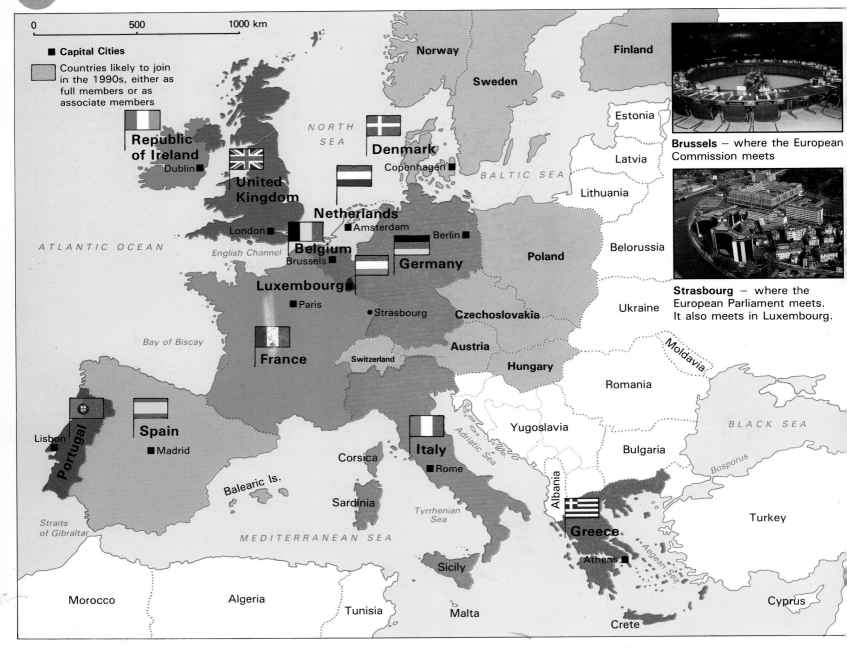

■ Capital Cities

Countries likely to join in the 1990s, either as full members or as associate members

Brussels – where the European Commission meets

Strasbourg – where the European Parliament meets. It also meets in Luxembourg.

Population
in millions

Luxembourg	0.38
Republic of Ireland	3.5
Denmark	5.1
Greece	10
Belgium	10
Portugal	10.4
Netherlands	14.9
Spain	39.6
France	56.7
United Kingdom	57.4
Italy	57.5
Germany	79.1

Size of the countries
in thousands of square kilometres (km²)

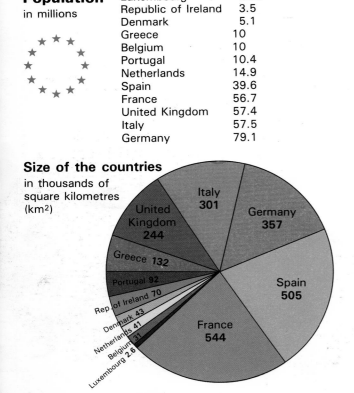

Italy **301**
Germany **357**
United Kingdom **244**
Greece **132**
Portugal **92**
Rep of Ireland **70**
Denmark **43**
Netherlands **41**
Belgium **31**
Luxembourg **2.6**
Spain **505**
France **544**

European high-speed road and rail system in the 1990s

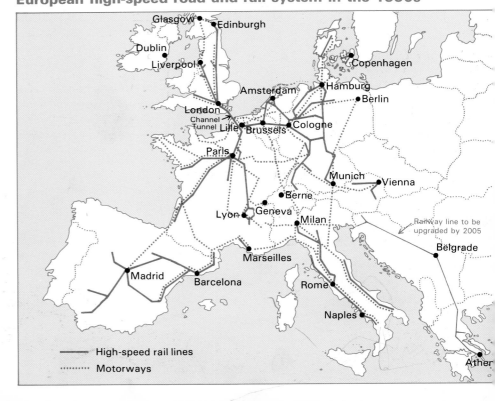

Glasgow • Edinburgh
Dublin
Liverpool
Copenhagen
Amsterdam
Hamburg
Berlin
London
Channel Tunnel · Lille · Brussels
Cologne
Paris
Munich · Vienna
Berne
Lyon · Geneva
Milan
Marseilles
Madrid
Barcelona
Rome
Naples
Belgrade
Ather

Railway line to be upgraded by 2005

—— High-speed rail lines
·········· Motorways

he distance round the World
 40 075 km

More than ⅔ of the World's surface is water

Land

Water

Size of the Continents
in millions of square kilometres (km²)

America **42**

Asia **44**

Oceania **8.5**

Europe **10.3**

Antarctica **15**

Africa **30.2**

London

Europe

Asia

North America

New York

Beijing Seoul

Tokyo

Los Angeles

Shanghai

Tropic of Cancer

Cairo

Calcutta

Mexico City

Bombay

Africa

Equator

Equator

South America

Tropic of Capricorn

Rio de Janeiro

Oceania

São Paulo

Buenos Aires

● World's largest urban areas
(cities and surrounding areas
with 10-20 million people)

Antarctica is a separate continent almost entirely covered by ice. This ice represents 90% of the world's fresh water.

No one lives in Antarctica except international scientists who work at the research stations.

Mining or other development will not be allowed for at least 50 years.

0   3000   6000 km

Antarctica

Population of the Continents

Asia **2876 million**

Europe **715 million**

America **669 million**

Africa **555 million**

Oceania **24.5 million**

World population
How World population has grown and is growing.

6000 million people

5000

4000

3000

2000

1000

0

10 000 million?

Years 1850 1875 1900 1925 1950   1975   2000   2100

For economic reasons, many 'British' ships are now registered abroad. Only about 800 trading ships are British owned. The largest fleets belong to:
Japan (9830)
USSR (6555)
USA (6375)
Panama (5121)

Launching a ship at Hull

Almost 500 million tonnes of cargo pass through the seaports of Britain each year. Of these, 55 million tonnes pass through the port of London.

Loading containers at Madeira

61% of the seaport trade of Britain is with other members of the EC.
Almost 30 million passengers use British ports each year. Half of these pass through Dover.

Tilbury dock complex, London

Ports and shipping lanes

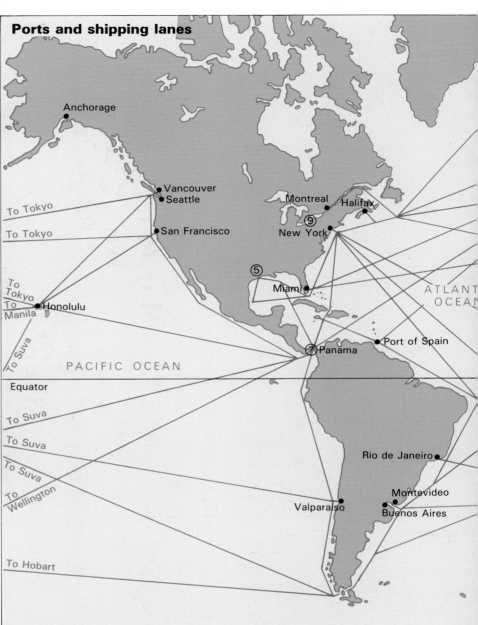

① White Sea-Baltic (formerly Stalin) **227 km**

② Suez **162 km**

③ V. I. Lenin Volga-Don **100 km**

④ Kiel (or North Sea) **98 km**

⑤ Houston **91 km**

⑥ Alphonse XIII **85 km**

⑦ Panama **82 km**

⑧ Manchester Ship **64 km**

⑨ Welland **45 km**

⑩ Brussels (Rupel Sea) **32 km**

Longest ship canals
(see map for locations)

Passenger ships

Cruise ship 'Cunard Countess' 17 586 tonnes 164 m long 750 passengers

Liner 'Canberra' 44 807 tonnes 249 m long 2400 passengers

Liner 'Queen Elizabeth 2' 67 936 tonnes 293 m long 2025 passengers
13 decks high, 9 engines, 5 restaurants, 4 swimming pools

Cargo ships

Refrigerated ship 14 000 tonnes 160 m long

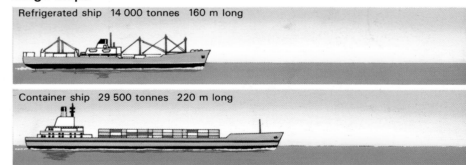

Container ship 29 500 tonnes 220 m long

Ore/Bulk/Oil carrier 170 000 tonnes 290 m long

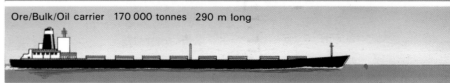

Oil supertanker 242 000 tonnes 380 m long 62 m wide

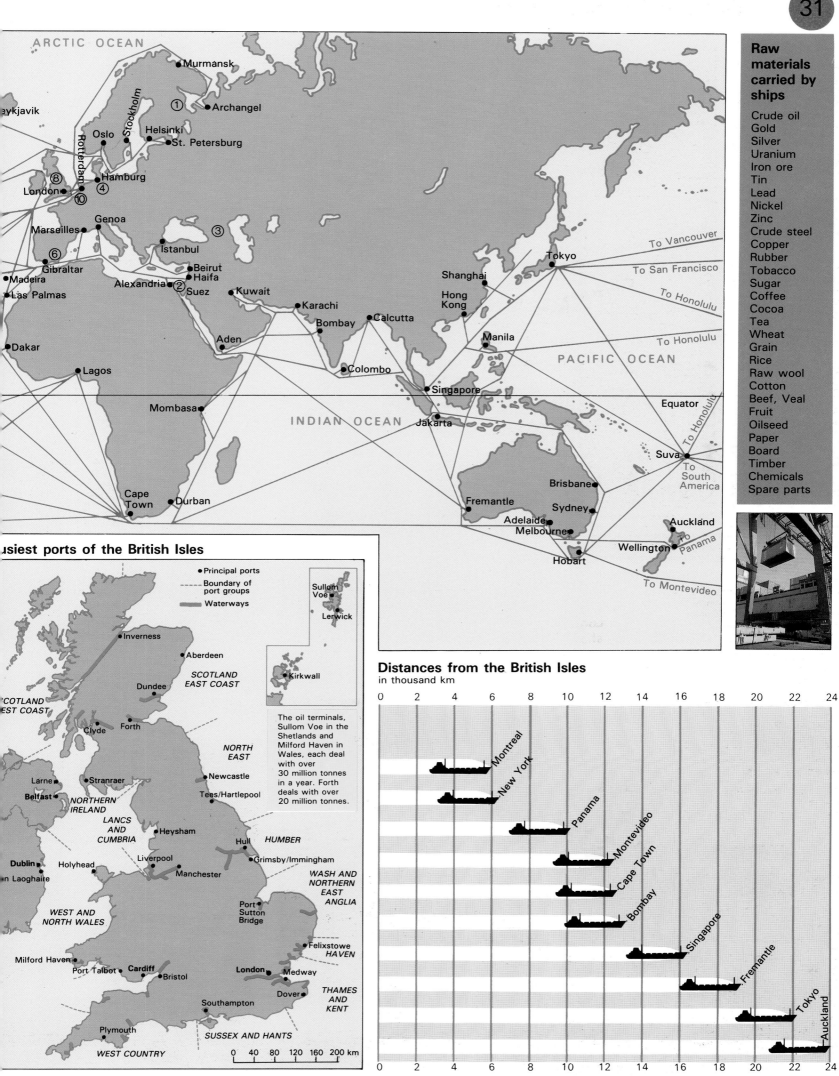

Raw materials carried by ships

Crude oil
Gold
Silver
Uranium
Iron ore
Tin
Lead
Nickel
Zinc
Crude steel
Copper
Rubber
Tobacco
Sugar
Coffee
Cocoa
Tea
Wheat
Grain
Rice
Raw wool
Cotton
Beef, Veal
Fruit
Oilseed
Paper
Board
Timber
Chemicals
Spare parts

ARCTIC OCEAN

Murmansk
Archangel
Stockholm
Oslo
Helsinki
St. Petersburg
Rotterdam
Hamburg
London
Genoa
Marseilles
Istanbul
Gibraltar
Madeira
Beirut
Haifa
Las Palmas
Alexandria
Suez
Kuwait
Karachi
Bombay
Calcutta
Aden
Dakar
Lagos
Colombo
Shanghai
Tokyo
Hong Kong
Manila
Singapore
PACIFIC OCEAN
To Vancouver
To San Francisco
To Honolulu
To Honolulu
Mombasa
INDIAN OCEAN
Jakarta
Equator
Suva
To Honolulu
To South America
Cape Town
Durban
Brisbane
Fremantle
Sydney
Adelaide
Melbourne
Auckland
Wellington
To Panama
Hobart
To Montevideo

Reykjavik
①
④
⑧
⑩
⑥
②
③

Busiest ports of the British Isles

• Principal ports
‑ ‑ ‑ Boundary of port groups
▬ Waterways

Sullom Voe
Lerwick
SCOTLAND EAST COAST
Kirkwall

Inverness
Aberdeen
SCOTLAND EAST COAST
Dundee
Clyde
Forth
NORTH EAST
Larne
Stranraer
Newcastle
Belfast
NORTHERN IRELAND
Tees/Hartlepool
LANCS AND CUMBRIA
Heysham
Dublin
Holyhead
Liverpool
Hull
HUMBER
n Laoghaire
Manchester
Grimsby/Immingham
WASH AND NORTHERN EAST ANGLIA
WEST AND NORTH WALES
Port Sutton Bridge
Milford Haven
Felixstowe
HAVEN
Port Talbot
Cardiff
London
Medway
Bristol
THAMES AND KENT
Southampton
Dover
Plymouth
SUSSEX AND HANTS
WEST COUNTRY

The oil terminals, Sullom Voe in the Shetlands and Milford Haven in Wales, each deal with over 30 million tonnes in a year. Forth deals with over 20 million tonnes.

0 40 80 120 160 200 km

Distances from the British Isles
in thousand km

| 0 | 2 | 4 | 6 | 8 | 10 | 12 | 14 | 16 | 18 | 20 | 22 | 24 |

Montreal
New York
Panama
Montevideo
Cape Town
Bombay
Singapore
Fremantle
Tokyo
Auckland

Weather areas of the World

Very cold All months below freezing point 0°C	Polar regions
Cold All months below 10°C	
Cool Warmest month over 10°C Coldest month below −3°C	Temperate regions
Warm Warmest month over 10°C Coldest month over −3°C	
Hot All months over 18°C	Tropical regions
Warm Warmest month over 10°C Coldest month over −3°C	Temperate regions
Cool Warmest month over 10°C Coldest month below −3°C	
Cold All months below 10°C	
Very cold All months below freezing point 0°C	Polar regions

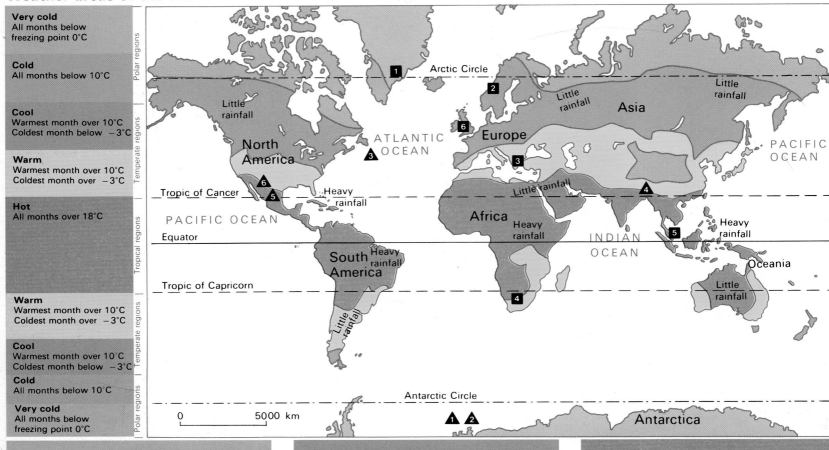

▲ 1 The South Pole has the least sunshine. In one year the sun did not shine for 182 days.

▲ 2 The lowest temperature ever recorded was −89.2°C at Vostok, Antarctica

■ 3 Grand Banks off Newfoundland has most fog. In one year it was foggy for over 120 days.

▲ 4 The most rain in one year, 22 990 mm, fell at Cherrapunji in Assam.

■ 5 The highest temperature ever recorded was 57.8°C at San Luis in Mexico.

■ 6 Yuma, Arizona, has the most sunshine. The annual average is 90% (over 4000 hours).

Different weather areas

1 Greenland (Very Cold　and Cold)

2 Norway (Cold　and Cool)

3 Greece (Warm)

4 Southern Africa (Warm　and Hot)

5 Malaysia (Hot)

6 British Isles (Cool)

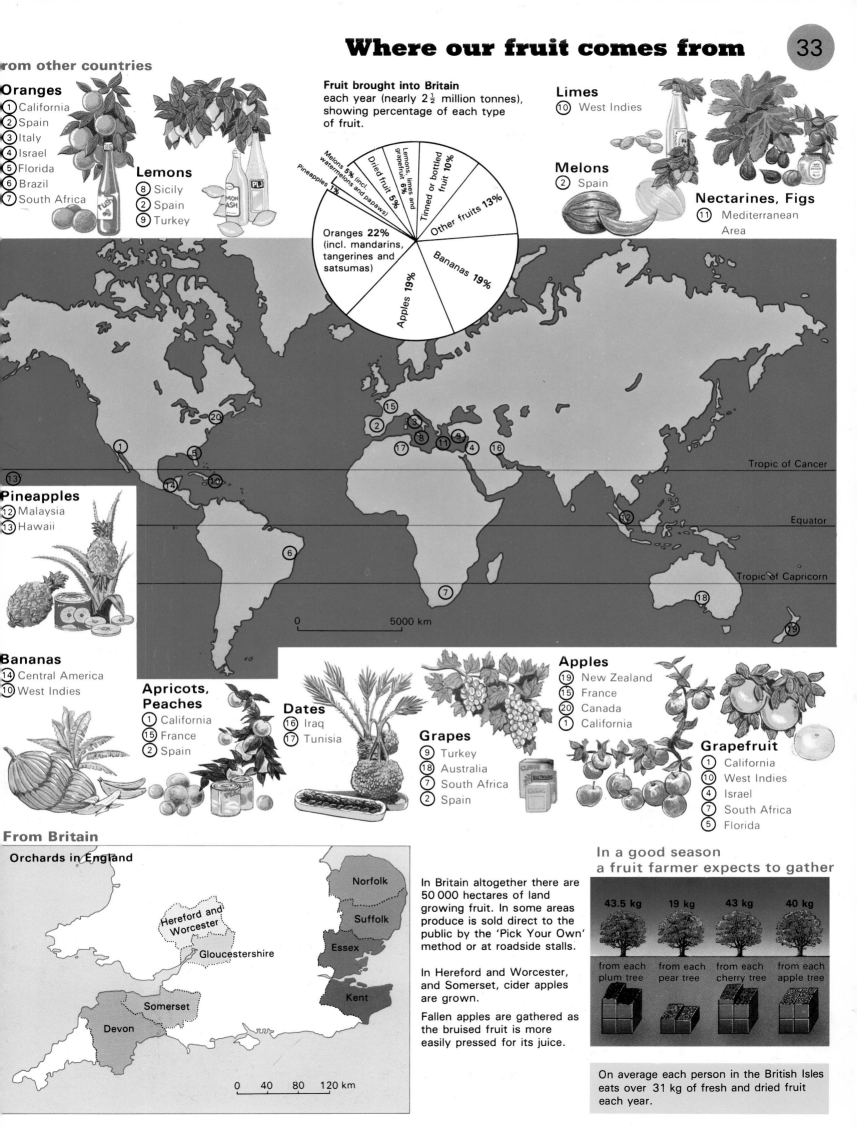

From other countries

Oranges
1. California
2. Spain
3. Italy
4. Israel
5. Florida
6. Brazil
7. South Africa

Lemons
8. Sicily
2. Spain
9. Turkey

Fruit brought into Britain each year (nearly 2½ million tonnes), showing percentage of each type of fruit.

Pie chart:
- Oranges 22% (incl. mandarins, tangerines and satsumas)
- Apples 19%
- Bananas 19%
- Other fruits 13%
- Tinned or bottled fruit 10%
- Dried fruit 6%
- Lemons, limes and grapefruit 5%
- Melons 5% (incl. watermelons and papaws)
- Pineapples 1%

Limes
10. West Indies

Melons
2. Spain

Nectarines, Figs
11. Mediterranean Area

Pineapples
12. Malaysia
13. Hawaii

Bananas
14. Central America
10. West Indies

Apricots, Peaches
1. California
15. France
2. Spain

Dates
16. Iraq
17. Tunisia

Grapes
9. Turkey
18. Australia
7. South Africa
2. Spain

Apples
19. New Zealand
15. France
20. Canada
1. California

Grapefruit
1. California
10. West Indies
4. Israel
7. South Africa
5. Florida

Tropic of Cancer
Equator
Tropic of Capricorn

0   5000 km

From Britain

Orchards in England

Norfolk
Suffolk
Hereford and Worcester
Essex
Gloucestershire
Kent
Somerset
Devon

0   40   80   120 km

In Britain altogether there are 50 000 hectares of land growing fruit. In some areas produce is sold direct to the public by the 'Pick Your Own' method or at roadside stalls.

In Hereford and Worcester, and Somerset, cider apples are grown.

Fallen apples are gathered as the bruised fruit is more easily pressed for its juice.

In a good season a fruit farmer expects to gather

43.5 kg	19 kg	43 kg	40 kg
from each plum tree	from each pear tree	from each cherry tree	from each apple tree

On average each person in the British Isles eats over 31 kg of fresh and dried fruit each year.

 Cereals

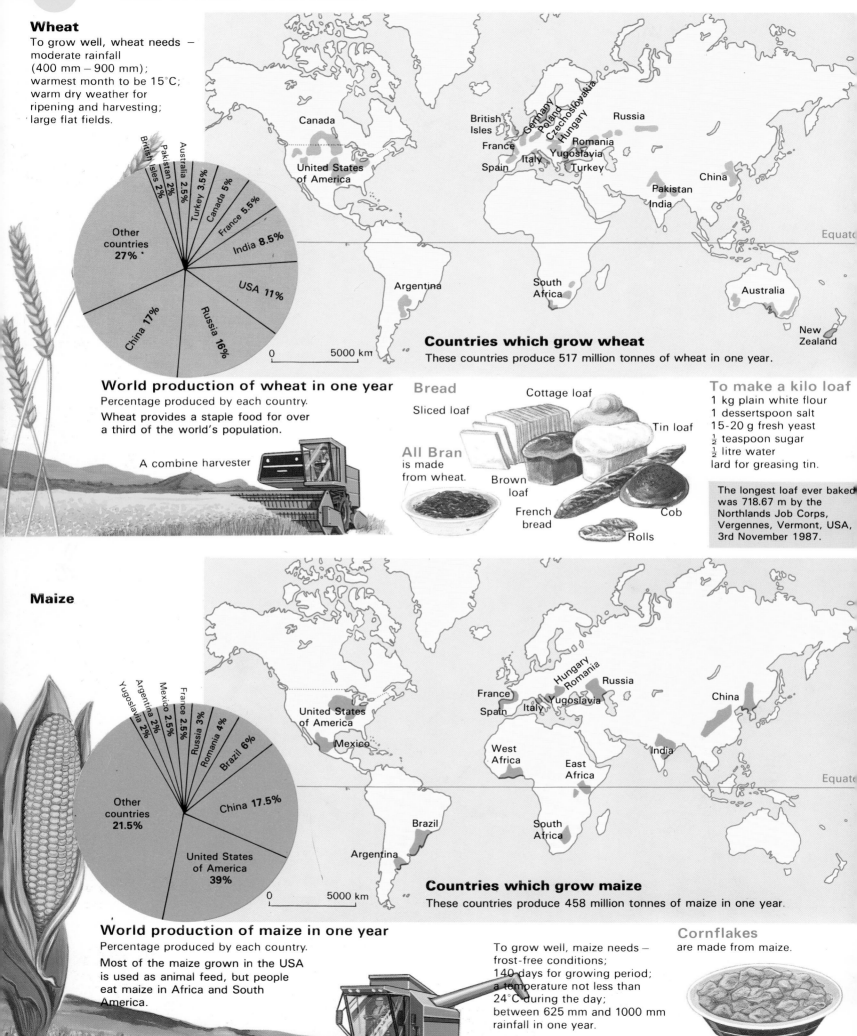

Wheat

To grow well, wheat needs –
moderate rainfall (400 mm – 900 mm);
warmest month to be 15°C;
warm dry weather for ripening and harvesting;
large flat fields.

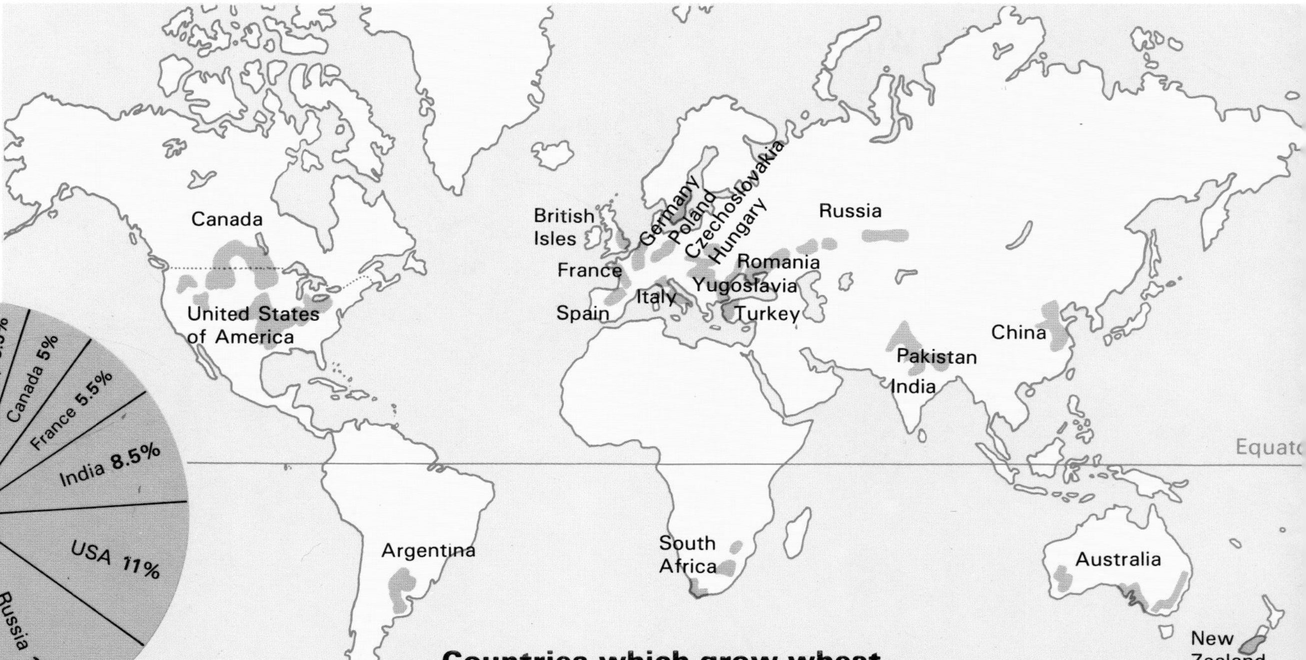

Canada
United States of America
British Isles
France
Spain
Italy
Germany
Poland
Czechoslovakia
Hungary
Romania
Yugoslavia
Turkey
Russia
Pakistan
India
China
Argentina
South Africa
Australia
New Zealand
Equator
0 5000 km

Countries which grow wheat

These countries produce 517 million tonnes of wheat in one year.

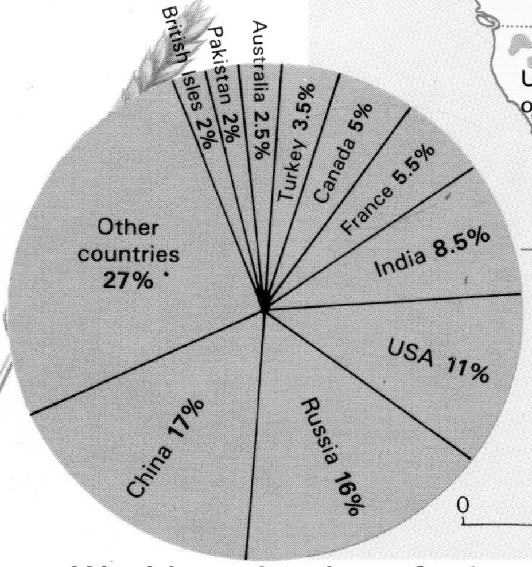

British Isles 2%
Pakistan 2%
Australia 2.5%
Turkey 3.5%
Canada 5%
France 5.5%
India 8.5%
USA 11%
Russia 16%
China 17%
Other countries 27%

World production of wheat in one year

Percentage produced by each country.

Wheat provides a staple food for over a third of the world's population.

A combine harvester

Bread

Sliced loaf
Cottage loaf
Tin loaf
Brown loaf
French bread
Cob
Rolls

All Bran is made from wheat.

To make a kilo loaf

1 kg plain white flour
1 dessertspoon salt
15-20 g fresh yeast
½ teaspoon sugar
½ litre water
lard for greasing tin.

The longest loaf ever baked was 718.67 m by the Northlands Job Corps, Vergennes, Vermont, USA, 3rd November 1987.

Maize

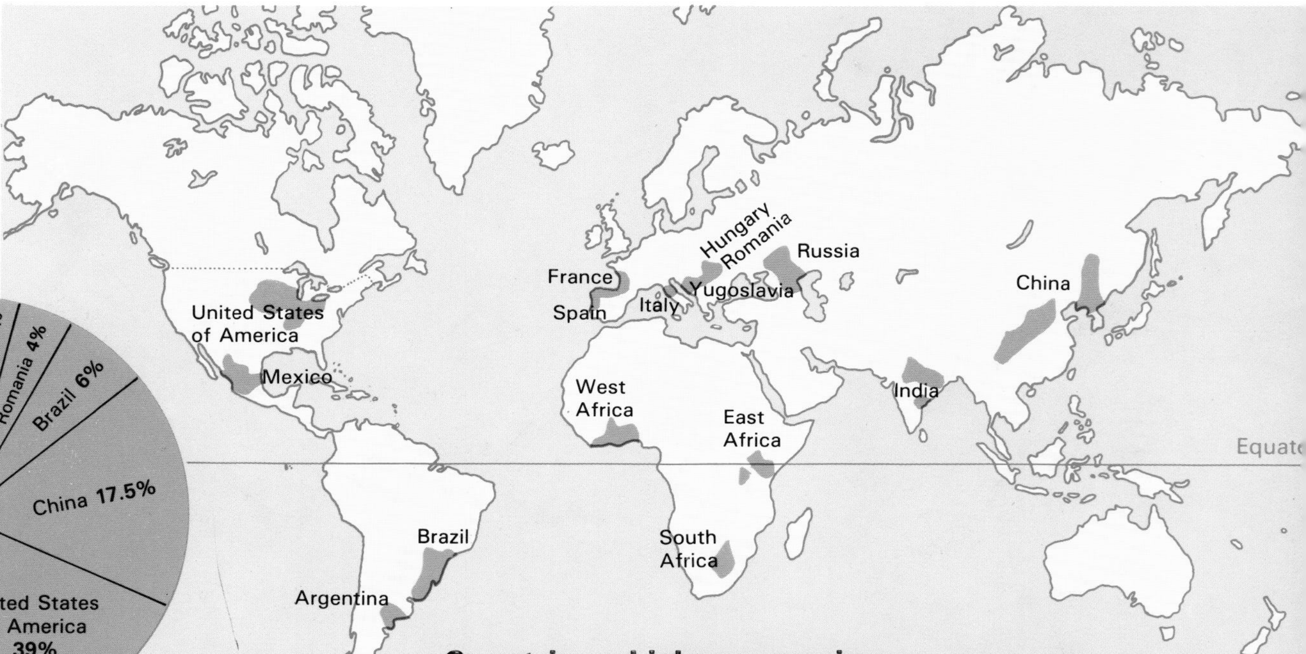

United States of America
Mexico
France
Spain
Italy
Hungary
Romania
Yugoslavia
Russia
China
India
West Africa
East Africa
South Africa
Brazil
Argentina
Equator
0 5000 km

Countries which grow maize

These countries produce 458 million tonnes of maize in one year.

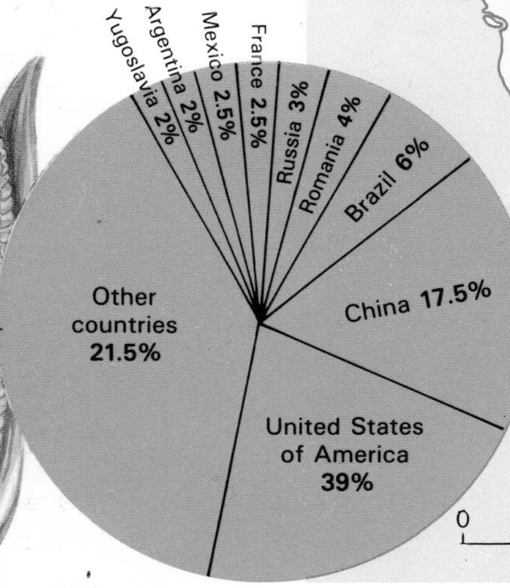

Yugoslavia 2%
Argentina 2%
Mexico 2.5%
France 2.5%
Russia 3%
Romania 4%
Brazil 6%
China 17.5%
United States of America 39%
Other countries 21.5%

World production of maize in one year

Percentage produced by each country.

Most of the maize grown in the USA is used as animal feed, but people eat maize in Africa and South America.

To grow well, maize needs –
frost-free conditions;
140 days for growing period;
a temperature not less than 24°C during the day;
between 625 mm and 1000 mm rainfall in one year.

Cornflakes are made from maize.

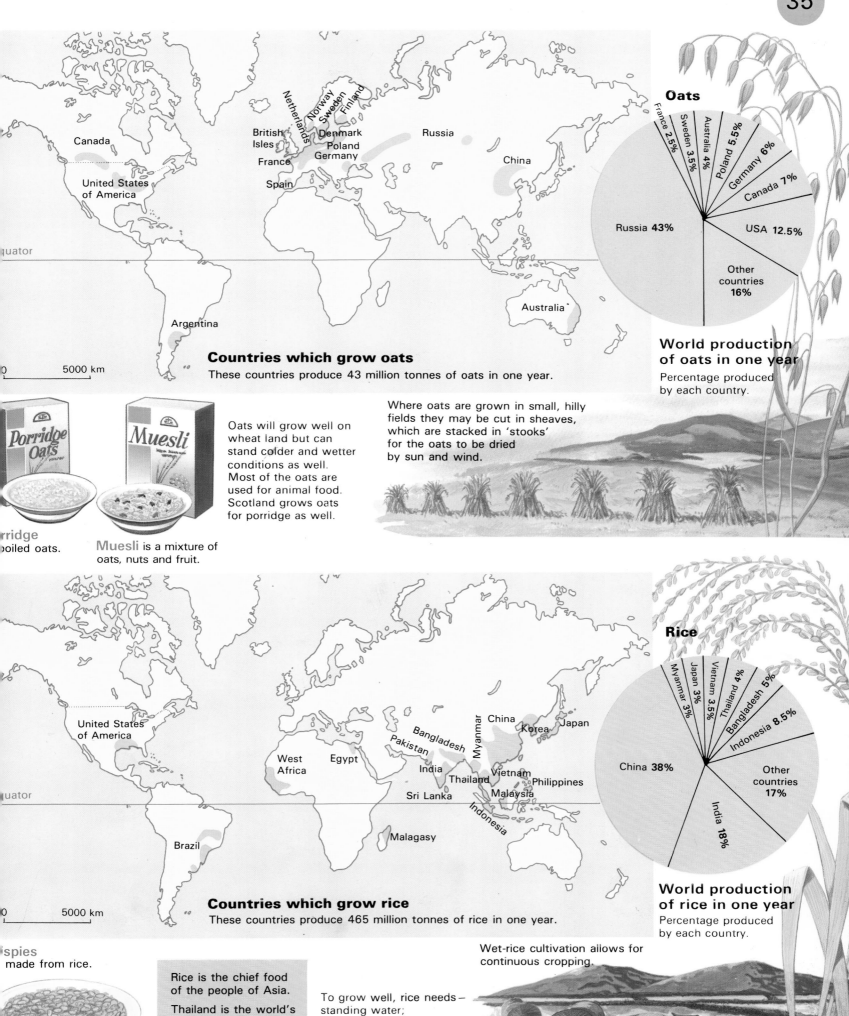

Oats

France 2.5%
Sweden 3.5%
Australia 4%
Poland 5.5%
Germany 6%
Canada 7%
USA 12.5%
Russia 43%
Other countries 16%

World production of oats in one year

Percentage produced by each country.

Canada
United States of America
Argentina
Netherlands
Norway
Sweden
Finland
British Isles
Denmark
Poland
Germany
France
Spain
Russia
China
Australia

Equator

0   5000 km

Countries which grow oats

These countries produce 43 million tonnes of oats in one year.

Oats will grow well on wheat land but can stand colder and wetter conditions as well. Most of the oats are used for animal food. Scotland grows oats for porridge as well.

Where oats are grown in small, hilly fields they may be cut in sheaves, which are stacked in 'stooks' for the oats to be dried by sun and wind.

Porridge Oats

Muesli

orridge
oiled oats.

Muesli is a mixture of oats, nuts and fruit.

Rice

Myanmar 3%
Japan 3%
Vietnam 3.5%
Thailand 4%
Bangladesh 5%
Indonesia 8.5%
China 38%
Other countries 17%
India 18%

World production of rice in one year

Percentage produced by each country.

United States of America
West Africa
Egypt
Pakistan
Bangladesh
India
Myanmar
China
Korea
Japan
Thailand
Vietnam
Sri Lanka
Malaysia
Philippines
Indonesia
Brazil
Malagasy

Equator

0   5000 km

Countries which grow rice

These countries produce 465 million tonnes of rice in one year.

spies
made from rice.

Rice is the chief food of the people of Asia.

Thailand is the world's leading exporter of rice.

To grow well, rice needs—
standing water;
high temperature, 20°C to 24°C; plenty of light; at least 1500 mm rainfall in one year.

Wet-rice cultivation allows for continuous cropping.

Cattle

In Europe most breeds of cattle are reared for milk or beef. As grazing is limited they spend the winter months in yards or sheds.

In the USA, Australia and Argentina, mainly beef types are grazed on the open range.

In less developed countries, cattle are used to pull ploughs, carts and wagons.

Hindus in India believe cattle are sacred animals and do not kill them or eat their meat.

Cattle give **beef** and many other products.

Cattle ranch, USA

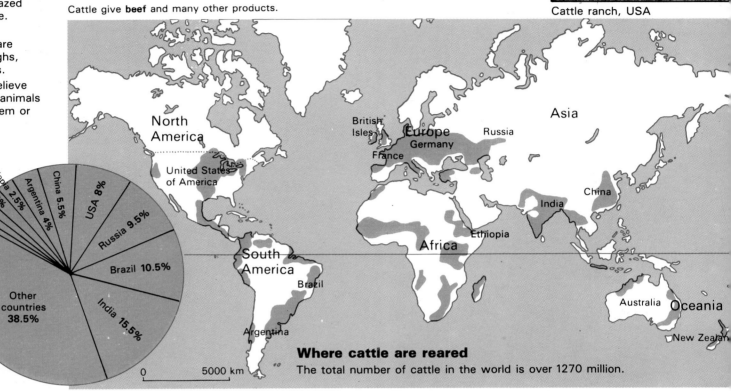

Germany 1.5%
France 2%
Australia 1.5%
Ethiopia 2.5%
British Isles 1%
Argentina 4%
China 5.5%
USA 8%
Russia 9.5%
Brazil 10.5%
India 15.5%
Other countries 38.5%

Percentage reared by each country

Where cattle are reared
The total number of cattle in the world is over 1270 million.

0   5000 km

Sheep

Sheep are reared for their meat or their wool or their skins.

They graze in open pasture which is most often found on hillsides where the grass is shorter and well drained.

Sheep can live without water for long periods of time. This allows farmers to rear sheep on dry plains throughout the world.

Sheep give **mutton** and **lamb** and many other products.

Australian sheep station

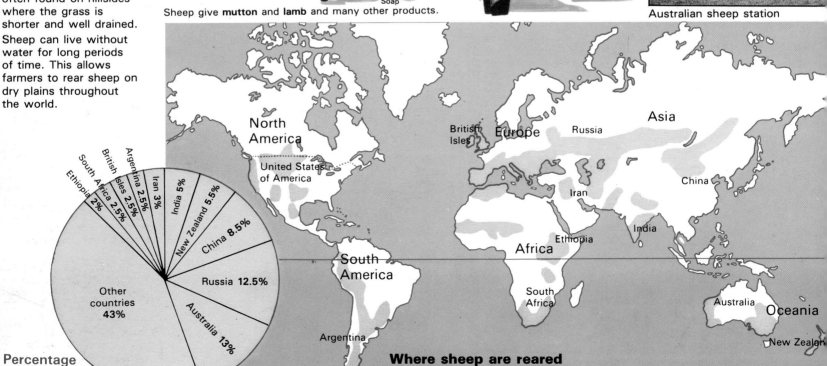

Ethiopia 2%
South Africa 2.5%
British Isles 2.5%
Argentina 2.5%
Iran 3%
India 5%
New Zealand 5.5%
China 8.5%
Russia 12.5%
Australia 13%
Other countries 43%

Percentage reared by each country

Where sheep are reared
The total number of sheep in the world is over 1150 million.

0   5000 km

Pigs

Pigs are often reared on mixed farms where they can be fed cheaply on waste products.

To grow well they must be kept warm and dry in special buildings.

In hot countries pigs like to wallow in mud because it helps them to keep cool.

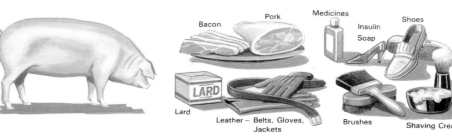

Pigs give **pork** and **bacon** and many other products.

Pig huts on a British farm

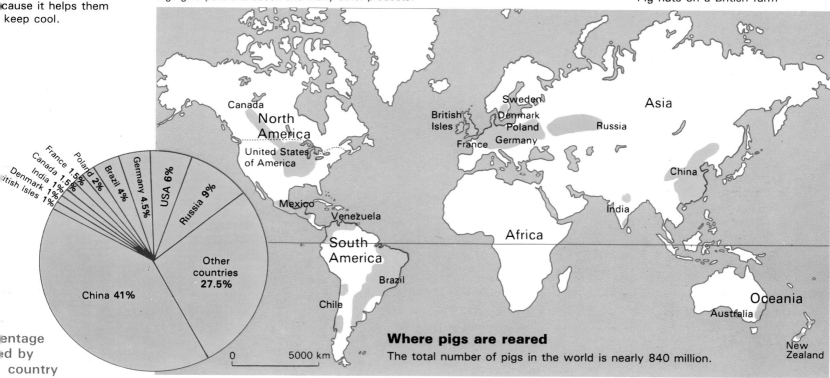

Where pigs are reared
The total number of pigs in the world is nearly 840 million.

Percentage reared by country

China 41%
Other countries 27.5%
Russia 9%
USA 6%
Germany 4.5%
Brazil 4%
Poland 2%
France 1.5%
Canada 1.5%
India 1%
Denmark 1%
British Isles 1%

0   5000 km

Meat from farms in the British Isles

- Beef cattle
- Sheep

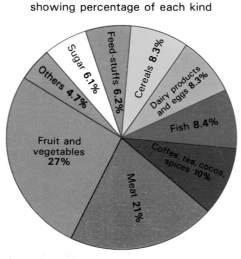

Scotland
Northern Ireland
Republic of Ireland
Wales
England

Meat production is carried on in most parts of the British Isles but it is most important in eastern and northern England.

Chickens and eggs

Most poultry meat comes from chickens.

Turkeys, geese and ducks provide smaller quantities of poultry meat.

Throughout the world more people keep poultry than any other livestock. The total number of poultry is over 6000 million.

Every year Britain produces about 1000 million dozen eggs.

Britain is self-sufficient in poultry meat and eggs.

Food brought into Britain
showing percentage of each kind

Sugar 6.1%
Feed-stuffs 6.2%
Cereals 8.3%
Dairy products and eggs 8.3%
Others 4.7%
Fish 8.4%
Fruit and vegetables 27%
Coffee, tea, cocoa, spices 10%
Meat 21%

Imported food represents 10% of Britain's total imports.

About 56% of the food on your supermarket shelves is produced by British farms.

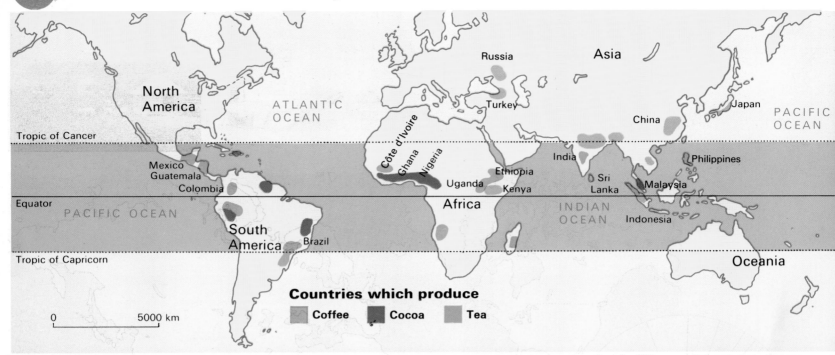

Countries which produce
Coffee Cocoa Tea

0 _____ 5000 km

Coffee
World production of coffee in one year is nearly 6.3 million tonnes.

Percentage produced by each country

Brazil 35%
Colombia 10%
Indonesia 6%
Mexico 5%
Côte d'Ivoire 4%
Ethiopia 3%
India 3%
Guatemala 2.5%
Uganda 2.5%
Philippines 2%
Other countries 27%

Cocoa
World production of cocoa in one year is about 2.2 million tonnes.

Percentage produced by each country

Brazil 18%
Côte d'Ivoire 30%
Malaysia 10%
Ghana 8.5%
Nigeria 6.5%
Other countries 27%

Tea
World production of tea in one year is nearly 2.4 million tonnes.

Percentage produced by each country

China 22%
Sri Lanka 9%
Kenya 6.5%
Turkey 6%
Russia 6%
Japan 4%
Indonesia 5%
India 28.5%
Other countries 13%

Coffee is made from 'beans' which are really seeds inside a red berry.

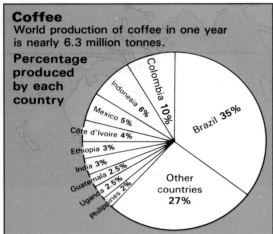

The ripe berries are picked from the evergreen trees which are 1.5 m high.

The coffee tree grows on tropical hills which rise to 2000 m. It needs a temperature of 20°C all through the year.

Maize and bananas are planted to shelter coffee trees from the hot sun.

The people of Finland are the world's greatest coffee-drinkers. They consume nearly 13 kg per person each year. For Germany the figure is 8.2 kg, for the USA 4.5 kg, and for Britain 2.5 kg per person per year.

Cocoa is made from the seeds of a 'cacao' pod.

A ripe pod would just cover the map at the top of this page.

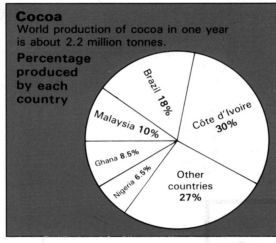

The cacao tree takes 10 years to grow 6 m. It should then give pods for 30 years.

Cacao trees need hot and wet weather all the year round. They have to be shaded by taller trees.

The beans are dried in the sun or in open sheds. They are ground into either cocoa powder or chocolate powder.

The USA consumes more cocoa than the other three largest consumers (Germany, Russia and Britain) put together.

Tea comes from the dried end-leaves of a tea shrub.

The evergreen shrub grows on hillsides in the tropics where there are hot summers and plenty of rain.

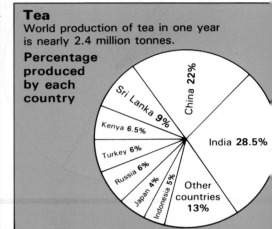

The end-leaves are picked off every three weeks.

Black, dry tea is packed in plywood chests which have a foil lining. Each chest holds 50 kg.

India is the world's largest producer of tea. It is also the world's largest consumer followed by Russia and Britain.

Tea merchants mix different kinds of tea together and sell the mixture as their special blend.

Sugar is produced from sugar-cane and sugar-beet

Uses of sugar

People in the British Isles eat, on average, about 42 kg of sugar per year. Much of this is in the form of manufactured foods, soft drinks and confectionery. Total consumption is 2.3 million tonnes, half of which is produced from home-grown sugar-beet.

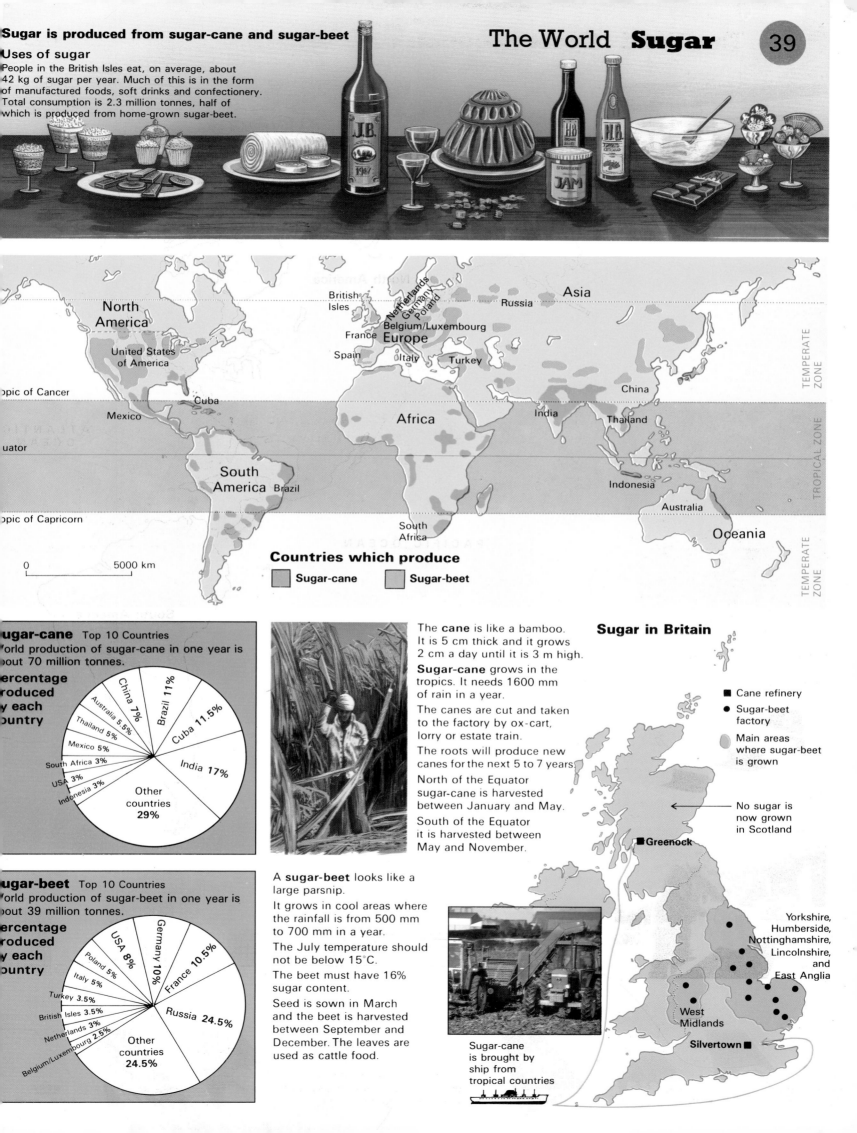

Countries which produce

- Sugar-cane
- Sugar-beet

Sugar-cane Top 10 Countries

World production of sugar-cane in one year is about 70 million tonnes.

Percentage produced by each country

- China 7%
- Australia 5.5%
- Thailand 5%
- Mexico 5%
- South Africa 3%
- USA 3%
- Indonesia 3%
- Brazil 11%
- Cuba 11.5%
- India 17%
- Other countries 29%

The **cane** is like a bamboo. It is 5 cm thick and it grows 2 cm a day until it is 3 m high.

Sugar-cane grows in the tropics. It needs 1600 mm of rain in a year.

The canes are cut and taken to the factory by ox-cart, lorry or estate train.

The roots will produce new canes for the next 5 to 7 years.

North of the Equator sugar-cane is harvested between January and May.

South of the Equator it is harvested between May and November.

Sugar-beet Top 10 Countries

World production of sugar-beet in one year is about 39 million tonnes.

Percentage produced by each country

- USA 8%
- Poland 5%
- Italy 5%
- Turkey 3.5%
- British Isles 3.5%
- Netherlands 3%
- Belgium/Luxembourg 2.5%
- Germany 10%
- France 10.5%
- Russia 24.5%
- Other countries 24.5%

A **sugar-beet** looks like a large parsnip.

It grows in cool areas where the rainfall is from 500 mm to 700 mm in a year.

The July temperature should not be below 15°C.

The beet must have 16% sugar content.

Seed is sown in March and the beet is harvested between September and December. The leaves are used as cattle food.

Sugar in Britain

- ■ Cane refinery
- ● Sugar-beet factory
- Main areas where sugar-beet is grown
- ← No sugar is now grown in Scotland

■ Greenock

Yorkshire, Humberside, Nottinghamshire, Lincolnshire, and East Anglia

West Midlands

Silvertown ■

Sugar-cane is brought by ship from tropical countries

Passengers

Top twenty airports
in millions of passengers in one year

Airport	Country	millions
Chicago	USA	56.7
Atlanta	USA	49.9
Los Angeles	USA	44.4
Dallas	USA	44.3
London (Heathrow)	England	37.5
Tokyo	Japan	32.2
Denver	USA	31.8
New York (Kennedy)	USA	31.2
San Francisco	USA	30.5
Miami	USA	24.5
Frankfurt	Germany	24.3
New York (La Guardia)	USA	24.2
Boston	USA	23.4
New York (Newark)	USA	22.5
Paris (Orly)	France	22.2
London (Gatwick)	England	20.7
Honolulu	USA	20.2
St. Louis	USA	20.2
Osaka	Japan	20.1
Detroit	USA	19.7

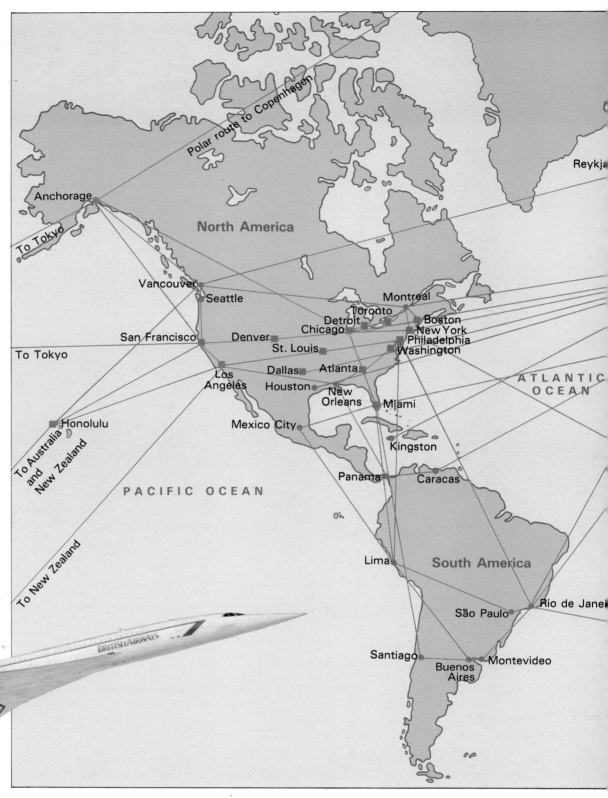

Concorde

Cargo

Top ten airports
in thousands of tonnes handled in one year

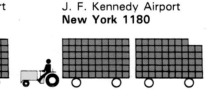

New International Airport
Tokyo 1203

J. F. Kennedy Airport
New York 1180

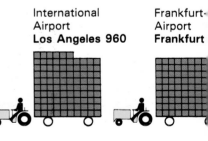

International Airport
Los Angeles 960

Frankfurt-Airport
Frankfurt

Airline symbols

Air Canada
Trans World Airlines USA
British Airways
Iberia Airlines Spain
Virgin Atlantic UK
Aer Lingus Ireland
Air France
Netherla

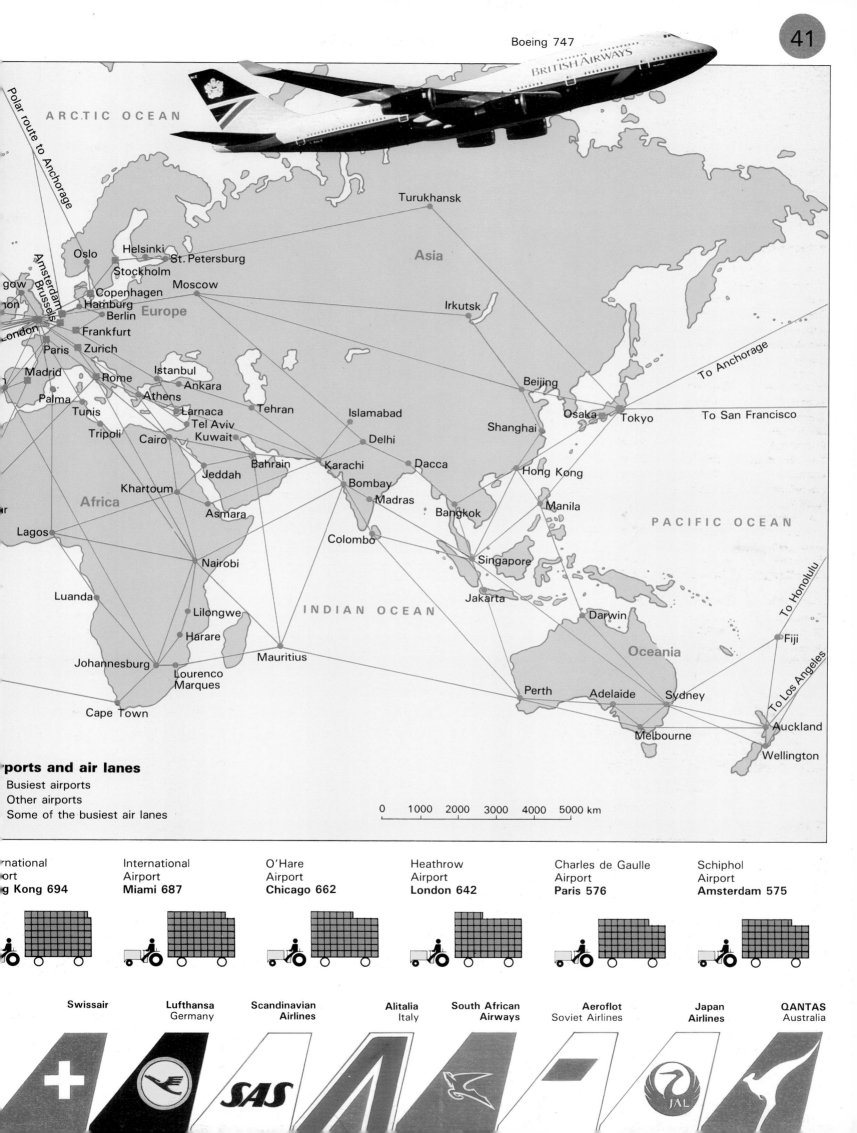

Boeing 747

ARCTIC OCEAN

Polar route to Anchorage

Oslo
Helsinki
St. Petersburg
Amsterdam
Stockholm
gow
Brussels
Copenhagen
Moscow
Hamburg
Berlin
Europe
London
Frankfurt
Paris
Zurich
Madrid
Rome
Istanbul
Ankara
Palma
Athens
Tunis
Larnaca
Tel Aviv
Tripoli
Cairo
Kuwait
Khartoum
Jeddah
Bahrain
Africa
Asmara
Lagos
Nairobi

Asia

Turukhansk

Irkutsk

Beijing

To Anchorage

Shanghai
Osaka
Tokyo
To San Francisco

Tehran
Islamabad
Delhi
Karachi
Dacca
Bombay
Madras
Bangkok
Hong Kong
Manila

PACIFIC OCEAN

Colombo
Singapore

INDIAN OCEAN

Jakarta

Luanda
Lilongwe
Harare
Johannesburg
Mauritius
Lourenco Marques
Cape Town

Darwin

Oceania

To Honolulu

Fiji

Perth
Adelaide
Sydney
To Los Angeles

Melbourne
Auckland
Wellington

ports and air lanes

■ Busiest airports
● Other airports
— Some of the busiest air lanes

0   1000   2000   3000   4000   5000 km

national ort **g Kong 694**	International Airport **Miami 687**	O'Hare Airport **Chicago 662**	Heathrow Airport **London 642**	Charles de Gaulle Airport **Paris 576**	Schiphol Airport **Amsterdam 575**

Swissair   **Lufthansa** Germany   **Scandinavian Airlines**   **Alitalia** Italy   **South African Airways**   **Aeroflot** Soviet Airlines   **Japan Airlines**   **QANTAS** Australia

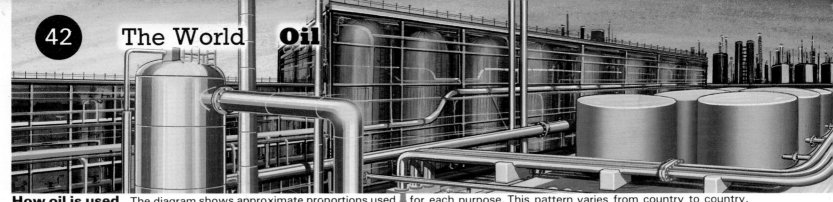

How oil is used The diagram shows approximate proportions used for each purpose. This pattern varies from country to country.

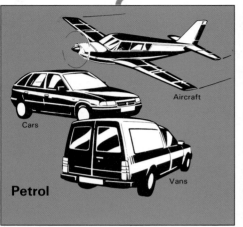

Petrol

Aircraft
Cars
Vans

Diesel fuel

Trucks
Trains
Ships

Jet fuel

Civilian Jets
Military Jets

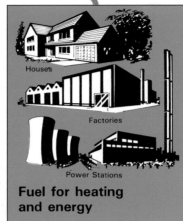

Fuel for heating and energy

Houses
Factories
Power Stations

Lubricants

Oils
Grease

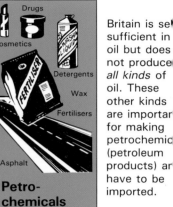

Petro-chemicals

Drugs
Cosmetics
Detergents
Wax
Fertilisers
Asphalt

Britain is self sufficient in oil but does not produce *all kinds* of oil. These other kinds are important for making petrochemic (petroleum products) an have to be imported.

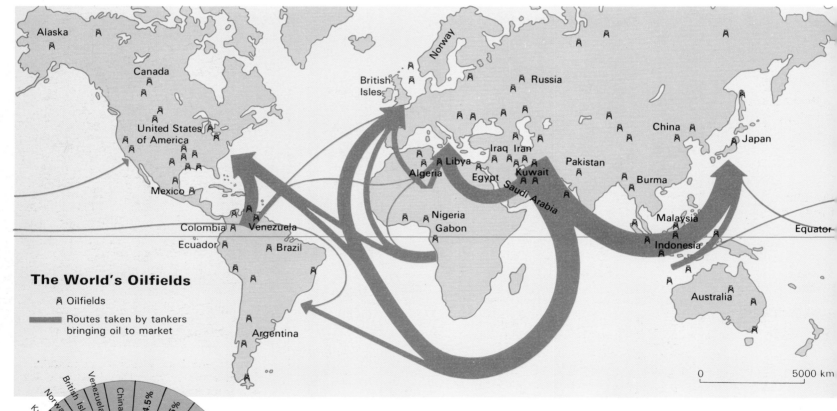

The World's Oilfields

Ⱥ Oilfields

▬ Routes taken by tankers bringing oil to market

0   5000 km

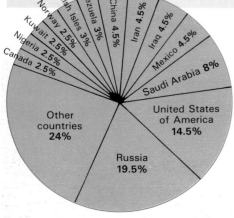

Percentage produced by each country

World production of oil in one year is 3200 million tonnes.

Venezuela 3%
British Isles 3%
Norway 2.5%
Kuwait 2.5%
Nigeria 2.5%
Canada 2.5%
China 4.5%
Iran 4.5%
Iraq 4.5%
Mexico 4.5%
Saudi Arabia 8%
United States of America 14.5%
Other countries 24%
Russia 19.5%

How long each country can continue to produce the large quantities shown on the left

British Isles	5 yrs	—
USA	10 yrs	
Canada	13 yrs	
Russia	13 yrs	
Norway	20 yrs	
China	23 yrs	
Nigeria	28 yrs	
Mexico	56 yrs	
Venezuela	85 yrs	
Iran	89 yrs	
Iraq	97 yrs	
Saudia Arabia	133 yrs	
Kuwait	162 yrs	

Even at a reduced rate, Britain will continue to be a major oil producer until well into the 21st century, long after the 5 years are up.

Oil supertar

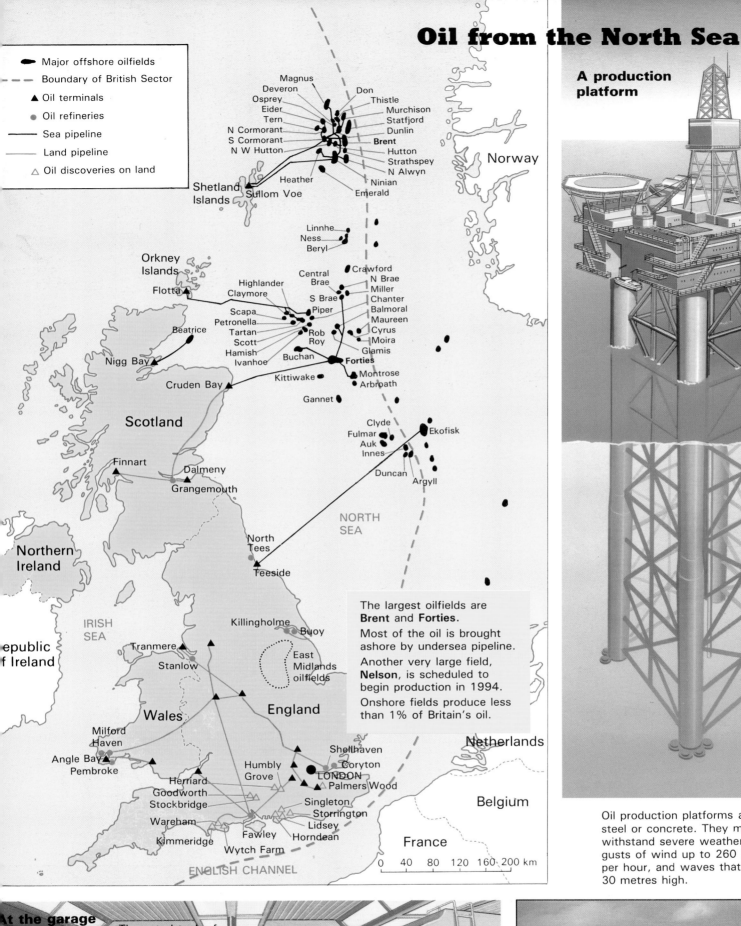

Legend

- Major offshore oilfields
- --- Boundary of British Sector
- ▲ Oil terminals
- ● Oil refineries
- Sea pipeline
- Land pipeline
- △ Oil discoveries on land

Magnus
Deveron
Osprey
Eider
Tern
N Cormorant
S Cormorant
N W Hutton
Heather
Don
Thistle
Murchison
Statfjord
Dunlin
Brent
Hutton
Strathspey
N Alwyn
Ninian
Emerald

Shetland Islands
Sullom Voe

Norway

Linnhe
Ness
Beryl

Orkney Islands
Flotta
Highlander
Claymore
Scapa
Petronella
Tartan
Scott
Hamish
Ivanhoe
Beatrice
Nigg Bay
Cruden Bay
Kittiwake
Gannet

Central Brae
Crawford
N Brae
Miller
S Brae
Chanter
Piper
Balmoral
Maureen
Cyrus
Rob Roy
Moira
Buchan
Glamis
Forties
Montrose
Arbroath

Scotland

Clyde
Fulmar
Auk
Innes
Ekofisk
Duncan
Argyll

Finnart
Dalmeny
Grangemouth

NORTH SEA

North Tees
Teeside

Northern Ireland

Republic of Ireland

IRISH SEA

Killingholme
Buoy
East Midlands oilfields

Tranmere
Stanlow

Wales

England

Milford Haven
Angle Bay
Pembroke
Herriard
Goodworth
Stockbridge
Wareham
Kimmeridge

Humbly Grove
Shellhaven
Coryton
LONDON
Palmers Wood
Singleton
Storrington
Lidsey
Horndean
Fawley
Wytch Farm

Netherlands

Belgium

France

ENGLISH CHANNEL

0 40 80 120 160 200 km

> The largest oilfields are **Brent** and **Forties**.
>
> Most of the oil is brought ashore by undersea pipeline.
>
> Another very large field, **Nelson**, is scheduled to begin production in 1994.
>
> Onshore fields produce less than 1% of Britain's oil.

A production platform

Oil production platforms are made of steel or concrete. They must be able to withstand severe weather, including gusts of wind up to 260 kilometres per hour, and waves that may be 30 metres high.

At the garage

The petrol tank of a family car holds between 40 and 70 litres, depending on the size of the car.

A delivery tanker carries 35 000 litres of petrol.

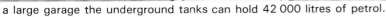

a large garage the underground tanks can hold 42 000 litres of petrol.

Grangemouth oil refinery

Softwood

Coniferous trees, many of which have 'needle-leaves' on short shoots.

These trees grow mostly in the northern (boreal) hemisphere in a cool, temperate climate. They require an average July temperature of over 10°C.

They can withstand low rainfall as well as heavy snowfall.

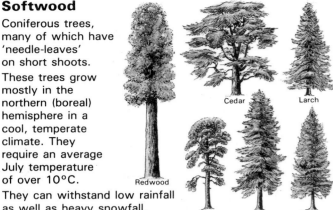

Redwood, Cedar, Larch, Pine, Fir, Spruce

Hardwood

Broad-leaved trees, many of which are deciduous and lose their leaves in Autumn.

Temperate hardwoods like oak and walnut need an average annual temperature of between 4°C and 18°C and annual rainfall of over 500 mm.

Tropical hardwoods such as teak and mahogany grow in frost-free countries and need at least 2000 mm of rain in one year to develop fully. The average annual temperature must be over 24°C.

Walnut, Birch, Maple, Mahogany, Oak, Teak, Beech, Elm, Chestnut, Ash

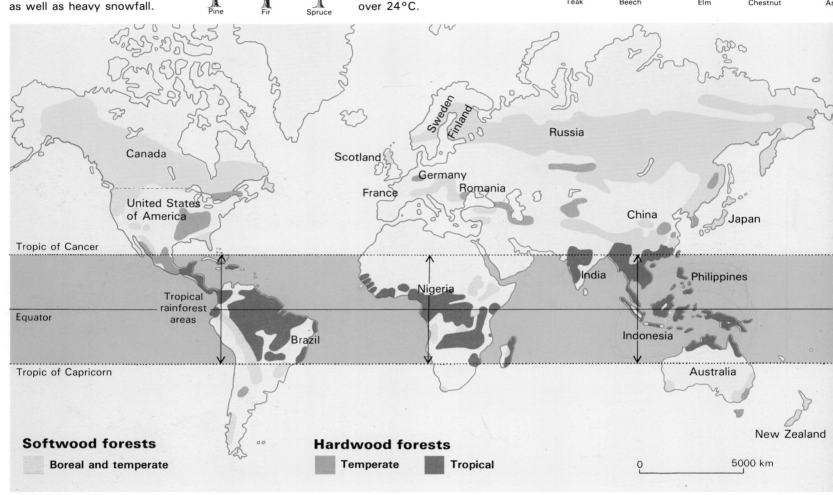

Softwood forests
- Boreal and temperate

Hardwood forests
- Temperate
- Tropical

0   5000 km

Softwood

World production in one year is 1360 million cubic metres (m³)

16% is used as fuelwood

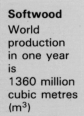

84% is used for industrial purposes, to make things

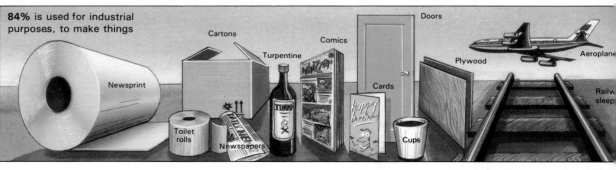

Cartons, Turpentine, Comics, Doors, Newsprint, Toilet rolls, Newspapers, Cards, Cups, Plywood, Aeroplane, Railway sleepers

---

Hardwood

World production in one year is 1974 million cubic metres (m³)

73% is used as fuelwood

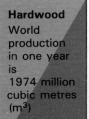    

The need for fuelwood is greatest in:
India
Indonesia
Brazil
China
Nigeria

27% is used to make things

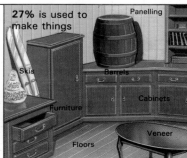

Panelling, Skis, Barrels, Furniture, Cabinets, Floors, Veneer

Note: The need for hardwood as fuel is a major threat to the rainforest. A further threat is the large-scale clearing of the forest for farmland. Only 10% of the hardwood produced is exported.

The greenhouse effect

1 & 2 Burning fossil fuels, such as coal, oil and wood, releases large amounts of carbon dioxide into the atmosphere.

3 Too much carbon dioxide prevents the Sun's heat from escaping back into space and so the Earth becomes warmer.

4 This 'greenhouse effect' could have disastrous consequences.

Changes in climate could cause widespread crop failures.

Rising water levels could flood some of the world's major population centres, if the polar ice-caps are allowed to melt.

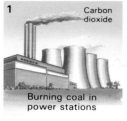

1 Carbon dioxide

Burning coal in power stations

2 Carbon dioxide

Burning tropical forests

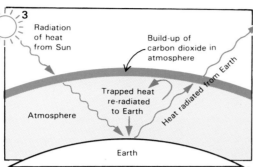

3 Radiation of heat from Sun

Build-up of carbon dioxide in atmosphere

Heat radiated from Earth

Trapped heat re-radiated to Earth

Atmosphere

Earth

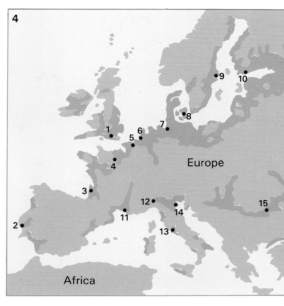

4

Europe

Africa

'Safe' land over 60m

Land at risk from flooding

• Major cities at risk:
1 London
2 Lisbon
3 Bordeaux
4 Paris
5 Amsterdam
6 Brussels
7 Hamburg
8 Copenhagen
9 Stockholm
10 Helsinki
11 Marseilles
12 Milan
13 Rome
14 Venice
15 Bucharest

Industrial pollution

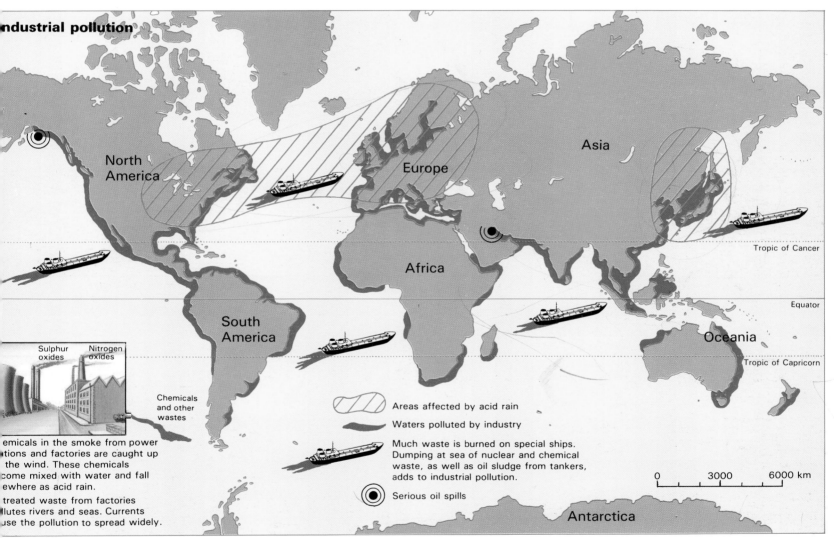

North America

Europe

Asia

Africa

South America

Oceania

Antarctica

Tropic of Cancer

Equator

Tropic of Capricorn

Sulphur oxides   Nitrogen oxides

Chemicals and other wastes

Chemicals in the smoke from power stations and factories are caught up in the wind. These chemicals become mixed with water and fall elsewhere as acid rain.

Untreated waste from factories pollutes rivers and seas. Currents cause the pollution to spread widely.

Areas affected by acid rain

Waters polluted by industry

Much waste is burned on special ships. Dumping at sea of nuclear and chemical waste, as well as oil sludge from tankers, adds to industrial pollution.

⊙ Serious oil spills

0   3000   6000 km

Some possible answers

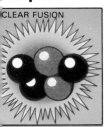

NUCLEAR FUSION

Present nuclear power stations produce dangerous waste. A fusion power station would be 'clean'.

GREATER USE OF HYDROELECTRIC POWER

Hydro power is 'clean' and still very underused. Countries like Malawi have great potential.

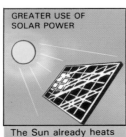

GREATER USE OF SOLAR POWER

The Sun already heats many of our buildings.

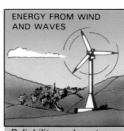

ENERGY FROM WIND AND WAVES

Reliability and cost are problems with this. Experiments are continuing.

POLLUTION-FREE ELECTRIC CARS

Manufacturers are already developing electric cars.

'CLEANER' FACTORIES

Factory chimneys are being fitted with smoke purifiers. Laws will prevent factories from discharging more waste than the environment can absorb.

Migration **Bird visitors to Britain**

Winter Visitors
4 Barnacle Goose
5 Pink-footed Goose
Golden Plover 7
10 Pintail
Whooper Swan 11
8 Ringed Plover
Starling 6
Bewick's Swan 9
3 Lapwing
Snow Bunting 12
13 Wigeon
14 Chaffinch
15 Fieldfare
North America
Asia
Europe
Africa
South America
Equator
Meadow Pipit 2
Blackbird 1
Summer Visitors
1 Swift
Swallow 2
3 House Martin
4 Willow Warbler
5 Whitethroat
6 Garden Warbler
Chiffchaff 7
8 Wheatear
9 Cuckoo
10 Nightingale
11 Yellow Wagtail

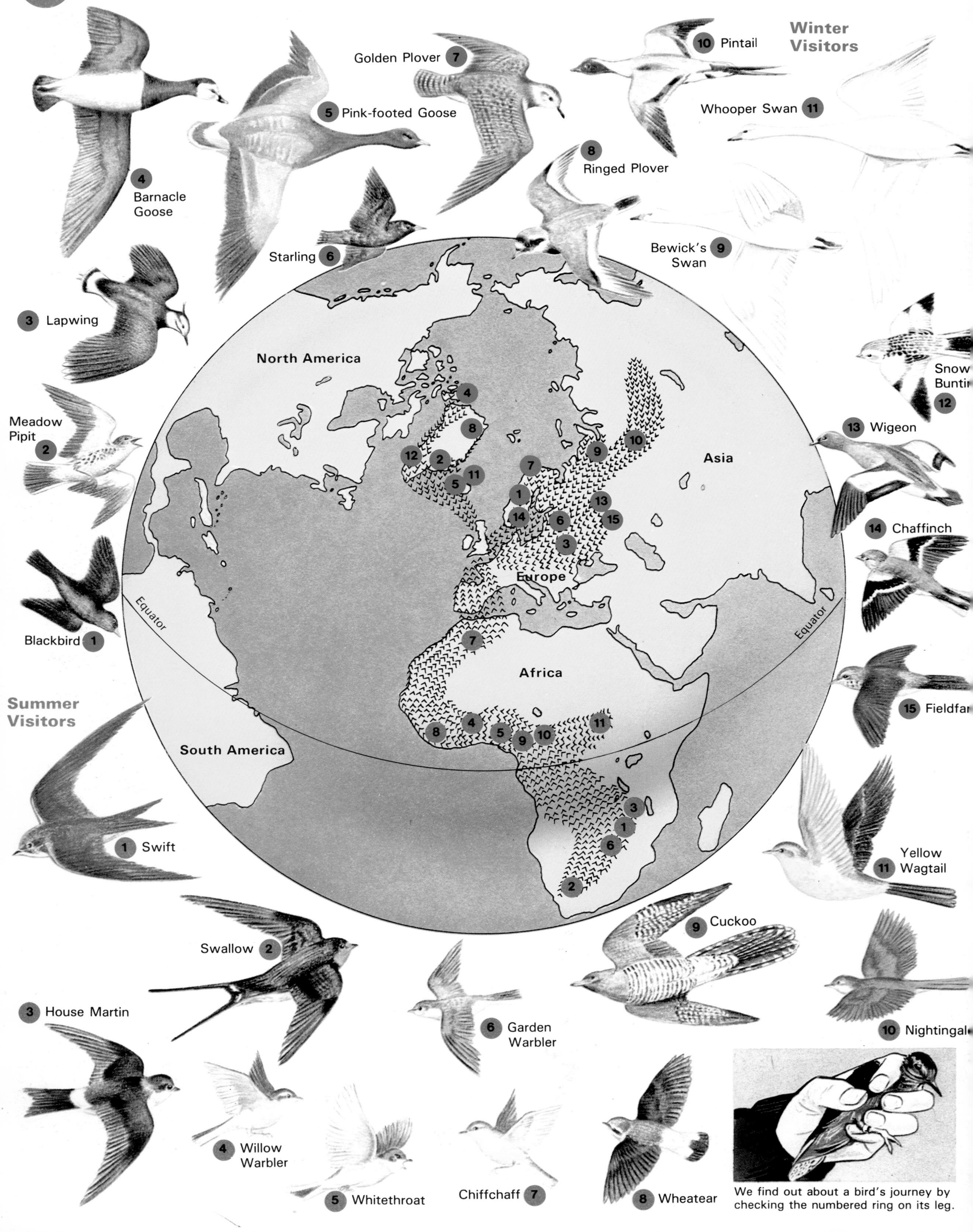

We find out about a bird's journey by checking the numbered ring on its leg.

North America

Kodiak Bear

Moose

Bison

Puma

Lynx

Beaver

Coyote

th America

Llama

Tapir

Jaguar

adillo

Anaconda

Penguin

Sea Elephant

Killer Whale

Antarctic Region

Europe

Red Deer

Chamois

Wild Boar

Wolf

Fox

Hare

Stoat

Badger

Otter

Africa

Giraffe

African Elephant

Hippopotamus

Lion

Leopard

Crocodile

Baboon

Gazelle

Gorilla

Zebra

Chimpanzee

Arabian Camel

Wombat

Arctic Region

Reindeer

Walrus

Polar Bear

Seal

Asia

Bactrian Camel

Indian Elephant

Mongoose

Giant Panda

Malay Bear

Cobra

Tiger

Python

Orang-utan

Koala

Oceania

Dingo

Red Kangaroo

Wallaby

Duck-billed Platypus

Acknowledgements

The author and the publishers wish to thank the following sources for permission to use photographs and other copyright material:

Satellite photo on title page courtesy of PLI/ESA

Sefton Photo Library, Manchester: pp. 7 (3), 8 (2), 9, 10, 14 (2), 16, 17, 18, 23, 26, 30

STB/Still Moving Picture Company: pp. 6, 9 (4), 16

The National Trust, Northern Ireland: p. 6 (Chris Hill for National Trust photo library)

Northern Ireland Tourist Board: pp. 6, 11

Bord Failte/Irish Tourist Board: pp. 6, 7, 11 (3)

Bwrdd Creoso Cymru/Wales Tourist Board: pp. 7, 10 (4)

Leeds Development Agency: p. 8

The Photographic Unit, Sheffield City Council: p. 8

Liverpool City Council, Promotion and News Unit: p. 8

Bradford Economic Development Unit: p. 8

Manchester City Council Planning Department: p. 8

Bristol City Council: p. 8

Matthew Gloag & Son Ltd.: p. 9 (Highland Park Distillery, Orkney — the world's most northerly whisky distillery)

Sea Fish Industry Authority: pp. 9 (2), 13

Aberdeen Tourist Board: p. 9

The Aberdeen-Angus Cattle Society: p. 9

Glasgow City Council Public Relations Department: p. 9

IBM United Kingdom Ltd.: p. 9

The City of Swansea: p. 10

Gulf Oil — Milford Haven Refinery: p. 10; also p. 42

British Coal: pp. 10, 19

Cardiff City Council: p. 10

Short Brothers PLC: p. 11

Waterford Crystal Ltd.: p. 11

Silverstone Circuits: p. 14

BEAMISH, the North of England Open Air Museum, Co. Durham: p. 16

British Gas plc: p. 20

National Power: p. 21

Nuclear Electric plc: p. 21

City of Dundee Tourist Board: p. 23

The J. Allan Cash Photolibrary: pp. 23, 26

Laing Civil Engineering Limited: p. 23

QA Photos, Hythe, courtesy of Eurotunnel: p. 23

Eurotunnel: p. 24 (map)

InterCity: p. 24 (3)

European Passenger Services: p. 24

British Airways: pp. 25 (2), 26, 40

Gatwick Airport Ltd.: p. 25

British International Helicopters Ltd.: p. 25

P&O European Ferries Ltd.: p. 26

Hoverspeed: p. 26

QA Photos, Hythe, courtesy of The Channel Tunnel Group: p. 26

P&O Cruises Ltd.: p. 26

Travel Photo International: pp. 26 (4), 27

Council of the European Communities, Brussels: p. 28

European Parliament: p. 28

The Yorkshire Dry Dock Company Ltd.: p. 30

Port of London Authority: pp. 30, 31

Reed Farmers Publishing Group: p. 37

ASDA Stores Ltd.: p. 37

The Sugar Bureau: p. 39

British Petroleum: p. 43

Special thanks are also due to:

All airlines featured on pp. 40 and 41
British Tourist Authority
Paul Burton, Burton & Burton Ltd.
The Department of Transport
Electricity Association
Bruce Hales-Dutton, Civil Aviation Authority
C. Holmes-Smith, the Timber Trade Federation
The National Trust
Mrs. Karen Sussex, MAFF Statistics Division
Mike Rolfe, MAFF Fisheries Laboratory, Lowestoft